THE
harmonious
CHILD

THE
harmonious
CHILD

Every Parent's Guide to
Musical Instruments,
Teachers, and Lessons

BETH LUEY *&*
STELLA SAPERSTEIN

CELESTIAL ARTS
Berkeley / Toronto

A Kirsty Melville Book

Celestial Arts
P.O. Box 7123
Berkeley, California 94707
www.tenspeed.com

Distributed in Australia by Simon and Schuster Australia, in Canada by Ten Speed Press Canada, in New Zealand by Southern Publishers Group, in South Africa by Real Books, and in the United Kingdom and Europe by Airlift Book Company.

Cover and book design by Betsy Stromberg

Library of Congress Cataloging-in-Publication Data

Saperstein, Stella.
    The harmonious child: introducing your child to music/Stella Saperstein and Beth Luey.
        p. cm.
    Includes index.
    ISBN 1-58761-171-6 (alk. paper)
    1. Music--Instruction and study--Juvenile. 2. Education--Parent participation.
    3. Music appreciation--Juvenile literature. I. Luey, Beth. II. Title.

MT6.S2547 H3 2003
649'.51--dc21

                                                                        2002031493

First printing, 2003
Printed in the United States of America

1 2 3 4 5 6 7 8 9 10 — 06 05 04 03

To the memory of my father

—BETH

To my parents, for their love and their songs
To my daughter, for making me a better teacher
To my husband, for believing in me
To all my past and present students and their parents,
for everything I learned from them

—STELLA

To all parents and children who want to bring
the harmony of music into their lives

—BETH & STELLA

contents

acknowledgments

We would like to thank the people who encouraged us and who read and commented on our manuscript: Dean Elder, Peggy Luey, Debbra Wood Schwartz, Marla Sheiner, Irene Tseng, and Ann Wolf.

preface

I grew up in a house where music was very important, though no one in the family was a professional musician. My father had wanted to be a pianist and, growing up in New York City, took lessons from a teacher with a studio in Carnegie Hall. As a teenager, he realized he would not succeed as a concert pianist and instead became a scientist. He continued to play for fun and also became an amateur conductor—most notably of a symphonic band composed of scientists at Brookhaven National Laboratory.

My father was my first piano teacher, and our lessons were not a success. I was too nervous and afraid of disappointing him, and I never actually learned to read music. When I was ten we moved to Pittsburgh, where I studied with two very good teachers (and finally learned to read music). My father and I played four-hand piano pieces—a spectacle that bore an eerie resemblance to one of Victor Borge's comical routines. I also attended a lot of concerts, mostly with my father. Several members of the Pittsburgh Symphony were close family friends, and music and talk of music were a constant presence.

I was not the world's best piano student. I didn't always practice, and to this day I occasionally dream that I have a piano lesson the next day and haven't opened my music. I got terribly nervous before recitals and was very relieved that my second teacher held only individual recitals for students who wanted to have them. But I enjoyed playing and never considered ending lessons. In part, this was because all of my friends also took piano lessons, and fooling around at the piano was built into our after-school social life. When I went off to college I stopped taking lessons, but

I still played for fun. My best friend was a talented flutist, and hanging out with musicians was an enjoyable part of college life.

My husband had studied piano throughout high school as well, and soon after we bought a large enough house, we bought a baby grand. When our daughter Nora was born, I assumed she would study the piano, though she picked up on the idea independently and a bit earlier than I expected.

Nora's lessons have taught me a lot about both music and parenting. Stepping back and letting her take responsibility for practicing was an important part of letting her grow up in other ways. I loved seeing her develop from the timid little girl whose playing was barely audible (Stella described it as "norissimo") to the teenager who rejected recital pieces as insufficiently flashy. I refused to let her end her lessons when she was eleven. I told her she would not be old enough to make such an important decision until she was fifteen, and by then she had no intention of quitting.

I cannot imagine living without music to listen to, and I cannot imagine raising a child without music any more than I can imagine raising a child without books and good manners.

—BETH LUEY

In 1979 I emigrated from what was then the Soviet Union to the United States and joined an international group of American musicians and music educators. Although it was frustrating at times, the experience was an interesting transition. Compared with a very rigid, disciplined, strictly regulated, and controlled Soviet system, the American music education system at the elementary level—mostly private, unregulated, and undisciplined—seemed to make no sense. At the same time, music education in U.S. colleges and conservatories is excellent, and schools of music such as the Curtis Institute, Eastman (the University of Rochester), Juilliard, and Manhattan produce world-class musicians. I asked myself, What and how can I teach and expect to achieve any results in one half-hour lesson a week? And what about separate lessons for music theory, solfège, the history of music, ensemble, accompaniment, or piano as a second instrument?

I felt very frustrated in the beginning and, like many of my colleagues from the USSR, I considered changing my profession. But that did not happen. What did happen, however, was that I evolved from being a strict and rigid graduate of a world-famous music conservatory into a more tolerant, patient, and flexible music educator. During the thirty years I have been teaching piano (ten in the USSR and more than twenty in the United States), I have taught hundreds of students ranging from the musically challenged to average to the very gifted. Never lowering my standards, I offered all of them the same level of my expertise and dedication.

What they learned depended on their ability, interest, and need. But I learned a lot. I saw the result of our work as I listened to them play at our class recitals. For some, it was a huge personal victory just to get up on stage and play in front of the audience—a victory over nerves. For others, it was a moment of glory, a time to share their talent, an opportunity to shine. A few times I caught myself thinking, "Hey, this really is not bad for one half-hour lesson a week and minimal practice. And don't forget: These students are not all selected for their musical gifts. They are anybody who wants to learn and who loves music."

Am I promoting mediocrity? I don't think so. I want everyone to have an opportunity to have music in their lives, and I don't want empty concert halls. As Eleanor Roosevelt recognized, "For a really healthy development of all the arts, you need an educated audience as well as performers." I learned not to compare my students with each other, letting them develop individually, at their own pace. None of this would have been possible in the Soviet Union's music system. Most of my students simply would not be accepted in the Russian elementary music school because they are of average musical ability, rather than extremely gifted.

I also learned a lot from my students' parents, especially the patient ones. At first I was in awe of their patience, those who didn't care if their children played the same piece of music for months (when even I was ready to give up). Later I started admiring their endurance. Now I use them as examples for those parents just beginning the journey with their children into the world of music. Be patient but realistic, encouraging but honest, and you will be rewarded with the sounds of music your children make.

Anyone can be taught music, but whether they become concert artists depends on many factors. Students who are not musically gifted, who are just plodding along, will never become great musicians, but they can become an appreciative audience and develop other important qualities—determination, self-discipline, and focus. Do we teach math only to the mathematically gifted? Or English only to future writers? Give every child a chance. Introduce music into their lives, sing and dance with them, encourage them, take them to concerts, and one day you will realize that your life too has been enriched by music, and that you have something very special to share with your children.

If my students develop a love for music, especially classical music, enjoy going to concerts, or just play and listen to music for fun and relaxation—and eventually share this love with their children—I will know that my efforts were not wasted, and that my mission has been accomplished. If among my students there is someone with an exceptional gift and star qualities, and I have the privilege of helping to develop this talent, I will consider myself very lucky.

—STELLA SAPERSTEIN

chapter 1:

WHY SHOULD CHILDREN STUDY MUSIC?

*I must study Politicks and War that my sons
may have liberty to study Mathematicks and
Philosophy. My sons ought to study Mathematicks
and Philosophy, Geography, natural History,
naval Architecture, navigation, Commerce and
Agriculture, in order to give their Children a
right to study Painting, Poetry, Musick,
Architecture, Statuary, Tapestry and Porcelaine.*
—John Adams

Imagine for a moment a world without music. The cave dwellers never noticed the sound made by their bows as the strings vibrated in the air. No one had ever carved a flute or stretched an animal skin into a drum. Monks never composed or chanted. Peasants and sailors never sang as they worked. Bach, Beethoven, and Mozart grew up as simple burghers. We have no symphony orchestras, rock groups, opera or ballet companies. You may have the blues, but you can't sing them. There are no jazz musicians, folksingers, or pop singers—not even a jukebox. Stores stock no music CDs or tapes, and all radio is talk radio. We have no national anthem, no film soundtracks, no musicals, no concerts, no Beethoven's Fifth, no "Over the Rainbow," and no "Imagine." Fred Astaire never danced, Luciano Pavarotti never sang, and Elvis Presley and the Beatles never scandalized adults or made teenagers swoon.

Music plays such an important role in our lives that we really cannot imagine its total absence. Yet very often, music influences us without our noticing. From the first lullaby to the farewell funeral march, music accompanies us throughout life, our one reliable friend, no matter what our state of mind. But even though music is omnipresent, we can enjoy it fully only if we learn about it and participate in it.

Music does not happen by itself. Someone composes it, and others perform it. Years of study and hard work—to say nothing of talent—go into the preparation of a professional musician, and very few people reach that level of accomplishment. But every life should include music. Even if we cannot all be performers, composers, or teachers, we can all become members of an educated, appreciative audience.

A Gift to Your Child

All parents want to give their children the intellectual, moral, and emotional foundations they will need to live happy, successful lives. Yet few things we can offer them will truly last a lifetime. We can give them a sense of security and confidence by providing love and support. We can give them strong values through our teaching and example. We can make sure they learn how to read, because that is the basis of almost all further learning. And we can teach them to appreciate and even create beauty.

Of all these possibilities, beauty is the most frequently neglected. And yet it is a part of life to which children are almost endlessly receptive. Uninhibited by adult concerns about talent and practicality, most children love to draw, paint, sing, dance, and bang away at any object that can create a sound. For them, the search for beauty is instinctive and spontaneous.

We believe that children can best develop their love of beauty by studying a musical instrument. This book is about the reasons we think this is important and the ways that parents and children can best benefit from music education. We have tried to answer parents' most frequently asked questions about choosing an instrument and teacher for their child, about starting and ending music lessons, and about practicing and performing. We have written about music education outside of formal lessons. We have also written about the fringe benefits of music education, including the ways it contributes to children's social and intellectual development. The book is arranged topically, but chapter 11 provides a chronological summary. We have provided a glossary of musical terms that we use in this book and that you and your child are likely to encounter in the early years of studying music.

We are not alone in believing in the value of music education. In addition to the musicians we quote throughout the book, there is enthusiastic bipartisan support for music education in the U.S. Congress. Senator Hillary Rodham Clinton writes: "Music education can help spark a child's imagination or ignite a lifetime of passion. When you provide a child with new worlds to explore and challenges to tackle, the possibilities are endless. Music education should not be a privilege for a lucky few, it should be a part of every child's world of possibility." And from across the aisle, Senator Rick Santorum notes: "Music education is an ideal tool for young people to develop the personal discipline needed to carry them successfully through life. Children learn about setting goals and persevering to achieve those goals through the process of taking a sheet of music, practicing that piece, and then mastering it to perform for their teachers, parents, friends and for themselves. This is an invaluable lesson in a culture that values immediate gratification over the joy that comes from a success born of disciplined, hard work."

Basic Beliefs

Our book is based on certain beliefs and assumptions to which we should confess immediately. Some of these have a basis in scientific and educational research, while others are simply our strong convictions. Our first assumption is that music is a basic and essential part of life. Here we have the support of the scientific community. Anthropologists have found musical instruments among the artifacts of the very earliest human communities. Even before they painted animals on the walls of the Lascaux caves, human beings played flutes and drums. The most recent research suggests that music (as opposed to an accidentally created pleasing sound) predates human beings, and that the songs of birds and whales follow musical laws similar to those followed by human composers.

Our second assumption is that music is omnipresent and diverse, and that understanding it better enriches our lives. From the time our clock radios awaken us until we turn off the theme song of the evening news, music surrounds us. In some cases, we have no control over what we listen to. Elevator music, "let me put you on hold" music, and waiting room music may be barely tolerable. But when we ride in our cars, work at our computers, or simply sit at home with access to a CD or tape player, we have a fantastic variety of music at our disposal. Most of us enjoy many genres of music. (Just think of the different stations for which your car radio is programmed.) How can we choose what to listen to? Even more important, how can we get the most pleasure from what we choose? Learning how to listen to music and to distinguish good music from the mediocre are skills that anyone can develop through music education. Music history, theory, and appreciation classes are all helpful. But actually playing an instrument enhances the ability to understand, to enjoy, and even to hear music. Everyone should be given the opportunity to participate in this, one of life's most basic pleasures.

Our third assumption is that musical talent is optional. You cannot aspire to a career as a musician without talent, but you can learn to play an instrument well enough to find it pleasurable and rewarding. A child can gain an enormous sense of accomplishment and mastery with only average musical ability. All the fringe benefits of music lessons—including the fellowship that comes from playing in a band or an orchestra—are available to anyone. And, of course, we can all learn to understand and enjoy the performances of musicians far more talented than we are.

Our fourth assumption is that music lessons are important enough to be taken seriously. You should take the time to think about your goals for your child's musical education. You should choose a teacher with great care. By accompanying your child to lessons, supervising practice, and arriving at lessons promptly and well prepared, you convey to your child that you appreciate the value of music as well as the value of the time devoted to it.

Our fifth assumption is that music is fun. Lessons may be the core of learning to enjoy music, but there is so much more! Listening to music on the radio, watching concerts on television, attending concerts, giving impromptu performances for friends, playing in small groups, singing—all of this is part of a child's musical education. Learning to play an instrument is serious work, but it is also the source of immense pleasure and joy.

Finally, we assume that music lessons will become an important part of your relationship with your child. Because music education contributes to your child's emotional, intellectual, and social growth, this is almost inevitable. Some of these interactions will be stressful. Almost every parent and child at some time will have conflicting ideas about practicing. The way you resolve these conflicts will depend on the kind of relationship you have with your child and on your own style of parenting. But these experiences can also improve your parenting skills and further develop your relationship with your child in a positive way. Music lessons can bring almost unimaginable joy to children and parents. Think about this: You have been listening to your child practice, and struggle with, a recital piece for months. If you have to listen to it one more time you will scream, and you think that you will never be able to listen to that piece with pleasure, no matter who plays it. Then—perhaps at home, perhaps at a lesson, perhaps at the recital—your child plays it with transcendent beauty. Such moments are rare, but when they occur, they are worth every wrong note that has ever hurt your ears and every argument you and your child have had about practicing.

We must also confess to a bias in favor of classical music—a bias that has an educational rationale. Sound classical training is the basis for learning to listen to and to perform all kinds of music. It is the best way to learn music theory and gain technical proficiency on an instrument. Jazz musicians build on these fundamentals in one way, classical musicians in another way, and pop musicians in another. No matter what your child's musical goals are, he or she will achieve them most efficiently by beginning with classical training.

Classical training is also an excellent way for anyone to overcome any insecurities about "understanding" classical music. Music—whether classical, jazz, or pop—is about enjoyment, not necessarily professional-level understanding. Musical training helps children hear more when they listen to any kind of music. It will teach them to understand musical form, to hear and appreciate harmony and modulation, and to bring their enjoyment to a more sophisticated level. Music education develops musical tastes and the ability to distinguish between a masterpiece and more mundane entertainment. If you are hoping that musical training will contribute to your child's intellectual development beyond music, classical music more than any other type offers the kind of complexity that researchers believe helps children's brains to develop (see chapter 2 for more on this).

This book is written for parents who want to give their children the gift of music. Like other gifts, this one will bring great joy to the giver as well as the recipient. If you know little about music, you can learn along with your child. If you know how to play an instrument, your child's lessons will present you with opportunities to reinvigorate your own love of music and perhaps even to resume your own musical education. We hope that reading this book will encourage you to bring the joy of creating and hearing music into your home.

chapter 2:

DO MUSIC LESSONS MAKE CHILDREN SMARTER?

Not everything that counts can be counted, and
not everything that can be counted counts.

—from a sign on Albert Einstein's office wall

Since the mid-1990s, newspapers and parenting magazines have asked whether listening to classical music makes children smarter. The discussion began with the publication of a study by psychologist Frances Rauscher and physicist Gordon L. Shaw, who had college students listen to a Mozart piano sonata for ten minutes. The students' spatial-temporal reasoning skills (which help with math) improved, but only for an hour. This bit of research, hinting at a possible shortcut to "smarter" kids, spawned a cottage industry of books and classical CDs that are supposed to improve brainpower instantly and effortlessly. Zell Miller, then governor of Georgia, convinced music companies to donate classical CDs to new mothers as they left the hospital with their babies. A Florida law now requires state-funded preschools to play classical music for half an hour every day.

It would be lovely indeed if listening to Mozart could raise intelligence, but it really cannot. Nevertheless, there are some more interesting questions we might ask: Can *playing* a Mozart piano sonata make your child smarter? Does it have to be Mozart? Does it have to be the piano? And, most important, in what other ways can your child benefit from playing an instrument—in addition to all the pleasure that can come from music?

Rauscher and Shaw conducted another study in which they divided preschool children into four groups. One group took weekly private piano lessons lasting about fifteen minutes, the second group took half-hour singing lessons five days a week, the third group had computer lessons, and the fourth group went to preschool as usual with no extra lessons. The children who had piano lessons improved their spatial-temporal skills significantly. A study on kindergarten children who took group keyboard lessons showed that they also improved their performance on tests of spatial-temporal skills. Apparently, playing works better than listening. This is hardly surprising: anyone who has taught or observed young children knows that active learning works better than passive observation.

Researcher Martin F. Gardiner conducted a study of first-graders in which two classes followed the usual sort of music and art curriculum, while four classes were taught using the Kodály method, which teaches increasingly complex music through singing. After seven months, the Kodály students had significantly outpaced the other students in math. Two years later, they were still scoring higher than their counterparts. We'll discuss the relationship between math and music in more detail shortly. Gardiner simply noted that music includes mathematical concepts and relationships, which may explain the children's rapid improvement. Some other studies have shown positive relationships between music and reading (especially if the reading teacher uses phonics) and between music and creativity.

The number of relevant studies is small. None involve instruments other than the piano, and we do not know what sort of music the piano students learned (though it was probably simple classical pieces or children's songs rather than jazz or rock). It seems quite likely that music lessons do have nonmusical cognitive advantages, but what kind and why are less clear.

Some people have observed anecdotally that students who graduate from high school at the top of their class often have studied music. Similarly, a large percentage of students who take music lessons seem to go on to selective colleges. It is not safe to assume that music lessons have somehow made these students smarter, however. For one thing, selective colleges expect applicants to excel in extracurricular activities as well as academic work. Students who hope to attend these colleges are therefore more likely to have studied music—if only to improve their chances of admission. It may also be true that "smarter" kids are more likely to be interested in music. In other words, intelligence may lead children to music lessons, rather than music lessons leading them to higher grades and test scores.

Another explanation has to do with parents. To the extent that music lessons reflect parents' commitment to their children's education and involvement in their children's lives, lessons contribute to the kind of performance gains that teachers and school administrators hope for. Other parents may show equal commitment and involvement in different areas, including sports or drama, and their children probably benefit in the same ways and for the same reasons. We believe, however, that music lessons have some real nonmusical benefits that other activities do not offer.

Stewart Gordon, a distinguished teacher and advocate of music lessons, points out that music lessons teach

- the perception and refinement of aural, visual, and tactile information
- virtuosity in abstract, conceptual thinking
- the ability to program and develop physical response
- the expression of emotion and attention to balance and individual identity
- how to deal with the preparation, disappointment, and triumph of performance

Because it contributes to such a broad range of learning, Gordon has written, music "has virtually no competition in any other academic discipline, or human endeavor." Moreover, he comments, "the benefits observed are applicable to every student, not just those who are gifted," and they "begin from the first music lesson."

Music and Learning

Whether music lessons make children smarter, we cannot say, but they certainly make them better students. To begin with, music lessons teach self-discipline. A child who has simply learned to sit still for fifteen minutes or half an hour every day begins school with a tremendous advantage. Children who practice an instrument daily have also learned to focus on a task, organize work independently, evaluate their own performance, report on their work to their teacher, avoid procrastination, and resist temptation. These may sound like extravagant claims, particularly when applied to preschoolers, but they are not.

Compare five-year-old Johann, who is practicing the violin, with five-year-old Barney, who is watching television. Both are sitting still, but there the comparison ends. Barney is not paying attention to his posture; indeed, he may be sprawled out on the floor. His eyes are focused on the television, but his mind and fingers may be otherwise occupied. He may or may not be thinking about what is on the television, and he may be eating or playing with a toy. This is not necessarily bad. Barney's engagement with the toy may be an imaginative extension of what he sees on the screen and may be much more intellectually stimulating than passive viewing. If something more interesting comes along, he may simply walk away.

Johann, however, is fully engaged in his practicing. He is conscious of his posture and of the way he is holding his instrument. He is looking at the music, following from note to note, paying attention not only to what pitch the note is but also to how long it should be held and how loudly it should be played. He is looking ahead to the next note or perhaps to the end of the phrase. He is also listening to what he is playing. Johann's mind is engaged, and so are his senses of sight, sound, and touch. Moreover, he has a sense of mission. He and his teacher have discussed his goals for the week and how he should practice to meet those goals. His physical and intellectual actions are purposeful.

Before Johann even began practicing on this day, he was exhibiting self-discipline and organization. He knew when practice time would start and (at least on some days) made sure to finish what he was doing beforehand in time to begin. (On other days, he just waited for a grown-up to remind him and then dropped what he was doing.) Perhaps with a parent's help, Johann tuned his instrument. He has, to some extent, planned his practice time. What will he play first? What will he work on and for how long? Will he play slowly or quickly? Will he try to memorize the piece? At the end of his practicing, he will put the violin away carefully, and (again with a parent's help) he will evaluate the session. At his lesson he will report on his week's work. In addition to self-discipline, he has developed the verbal skills necessary to describe his work to his parents and his teacher. He is beginning to set his own priorities.

Now, if you were a kindergarten or first-grade teacher, you would probably like Barney and Johann. They are both pleasant, happy, bright little boys. But which of them do you think is more ready to learn?

Paying Attention and Following Directions

Kindergarten teachers have some other reasons to hope they have a few children in class who have had music lessons. Try to imagine what takes place at five-year-old Amy's piano lessons. She has been studying piano for six months. We will not consider right now how much music she has learned. Amy may be a prodigy who is already reading both staffs and playing beautifully, or she may be an average student who is progressing more slowly. It really doesn't matter. In either case, look at what else she has learned. She arrives at her lesson on time (through her parents' commitment to leaving promptly, she has learned the value of punctuality), with her music, which she has gathered together herself ahead of time. If she has been eating in the car, she washes her hands before going to the piano. She says good morning to her teacher and tells her about her practicing, articulating both her accomplishments and her remaining problems (and perhaps confessing to a bit of negligence). She then plays something. Next, she listens to what her teacher has to say. She pays attention to her teacher's words, her explanations of musical ideas, and her demonstrations at the keyboard. She may play together with her teacher. If so, she listens to both pianos and tries to match her playing with that of her teacher. She follows directions, asks and answers questions, and engages intellectually with an adult. She pays attention to instructions for practicing during the coming week. She waits for her teacher to tell her when her lesson is over, gathers up her music, and says good-bye. (Please note that not every lesson goes this well. There are days when Amy's teacher wonders why she didn't take up lion taming.)

These are all extremely important learning skills. To succeed in school, young children must learn to pay attention to time (arrive on time, be conscious of how much time remains to accomplish a task, leave time to clean up, etc.), to come prepared for school (with pencils, crayons, or whatever they are supposed to bring), and to adapt to a schedule. They must interact attentively and politely with adults.

Perhaps most important, they must learn to listen—to themselves, to other children, to stories being read, and to teachers. If music lessons teach nothing else, they teach children to listen in a very active way. As children play, they listen to the music they make. They learn to enjoy listening, to discriminate, and to hear and correct errors. They learn to compare the teacher's performance with their own, and to compare their own perfor-mances over time. Schools expect children to "listen" in the sense of paying attention and following directions. But children learn many other things through the kind of listening that music teaches. They learn to listen as they read aloud and to compare their own reading with that of the teacher. They learn to discriminate between correct and incorrect grammar and pronunciation by listening attentively. They may even learn to "listen" more sensitively to the emotional nuances in other people's speech. Again, these may sound like extravagant claims to make for a five-year-old. Talk to an experienced teacher, though, and you will discover how important these skills are to a child's success—and the different ways that children can develop them.

Playing a musical instrument also improves motor skills and coordination. Playing the violin, piano, flute, or other instrument requires children to move their fingers and hands independently, to develop strength in large and small muscles, and to coordinate fingers, hands, and sometimes feet. Parents report that music lessons lead to more legible handwriting and improved use of silverware.

Older Children

Music lessons can also contribute to learning skills that older children need. Even teenagers (who presumably can sit still, pay attention, and respond to adults, although they may choose not to) can develop skills in their music lessons that will help them with their increasingly demanding schoolwork. Let's begin with basic study habits. To excel in high school, students must be able to handle a large volume of homework and to balance this with extracurricular activities, additional domestic responsibilities, a social life independent of their parents, and perhaps a part-time job. They also tend to need more sleep. Study and time-management skills are vital.

When Johann and Amy reach high school, they will already possess some of these skills. As we have seen, they know something about scheduling, about planning their work, and about spending time in a purposeful way. Over the past eight or nine years, they will have developed those skills extensively. They will now be practicing at least an hour a day, having built up to that practice time gradually since middle school. Johann, in fact, will be practicing more than that, because in addition to his lessons, he will have orchestra music to master. Amy and Johann will have learned to increase the amount and intensity of their practicing before recitals and competitions.

These young musicians will have transferred their skills at organizing their practice time and making it purposeful to managing their homework time. At the beginning of each week, Johann and Amy will look at what is on their school schedule, and they will plan when to do homework, when to practice, and when to do other things. They will make allowances for slacking off and for social opportunities that are too good to pass up. When they sit down to do their homework, it will not be in front of the television. They will find a quiet place with no distractions, they will know what they have to get done, and they will do it in an organized and purposeful way. They will know when to ask for help. If they need to go to the library, they will not announce this half an hour before the library closes to a parent who is getting ready for bed. They will let their parents know ahead of time, and when they get to the library they will know what they are looking for.

The skills Johann and Amy have learned in preparing for performances will stand them in good stead when they have long-term projects or final exams. They will begin preparing ahead of time, and they will know how to handle nervousness or panic. They will not be timid about giving oral reports. They will be able to discuss their scheduling or other problems with school counselors and administrators without getting anxious or being obnoxious. They will have developed poise and confidence that their teachers will appreciate, their friends' parents will marvel at, and their own parents will find hard to credit. As Stewart Gordon has noted, "Music making is one of the best training grounds for learning how to prepare for performance, for meeting its stress and challenges, for learning how to deal with both the short-range disappointments and successes, and for mapping out a strategy for long-range achievement."

High school students need to develop certain skills to which music lessons can contribute. Every student nowadays must learn to use a computer. The dexterity that young musicians develop makes using a keyboard and a mouse extraordinarily easy. Pianists especially develop phenomenal typing speed in just a few weeks. Teenagers often become clumsy in gross motor activities—they trip easily and drop things. But if music lessons have helped them to develop the kind of dexterity that involves small muscles, like those in their hands, this survives adolescent ineptitude.

Far more important is the ability to memorize. People like to think that education has developed to the point where students' abilities to think logically and creatively are of the highest value, and that rote memorization is passé. In fact, even if students think very logically and creatively, most subjects also require that they know some facts, which have to be memorized. You cannot do well in math, chemistry, biology, physics, history, economics, government, English, a foreign language, or drama if you cannot memorize. Similarly, you cannot play most sports well if you cannot memorize rules and strategy. Woody Allen once claimed that 80 percent of life is showing up. We say the rest may be memorizing.

Children who take music lessons begin memorizing right away. They may not have conscious, formal strategies for memorizing. Most children just play their pieces over and over until they are (seemingly magically) committed to memory. Other young students are more systematic. Some teachers have special methods for helping children to learn their pieces by heart. Memorization by repetition does not develop more complex learning skills, as other systems do. Learning to memorize analytically, as teachers encourage, develops the ability to memorize words, formulas, images, and stage directions. Analytical systems develop a variety of memory skills rather than relying on motoric memory alone. Just as playing music somehow makes students better puzzle solvers and phonetic readers, memorizing music makes them better rememberers.

Sometimes music helps memorization directly. Children who play music often listen to music as they study. This is pleasurable, shuts out distractions, and may facilitate the learning of academic material. It also gives them a way to associate material to be memorized (perhaps chemical formulas) with music, which uses the hearing part of the brain. Sometimes all children have to do to recall a sequence of equations is summon up the Chopin prelude they listened to while they were learning it.

Music and Mathematics

Many people have noticed that musicians tend to be good at math, and that mathematicians are often amateur musicians or at least avid concertgoers. The affinity between the two subjects is fascinating. Edward Rothstein discusses this relationship in his marvelous book *Emblems of Mind: The Inner Life of Music and Mathematics*. If you are interested in a contemplative, rich view of these two subjects, you will want to read it. In this chapter, though, we are going to talk only about the relationships that are important to children's learning.

Children learn mathematics by beginning with the concrete and moving to the abstract. The concrete may be fingers, blocks, beads, raisins, or almost anything that they can see and touch. Depending on the way math is taught, they may spend a great deal of time at the concrete level before switching to the abstraction of numbers. (Although we may not think of this very often, arabic numerals like 4 are abstractions, symbolic representations of quantities.) Some children learn to add, subtract, multiply, and divide with beads before they are taught to use numerals. Music is also both abstract and concrete in its use of numbers. A ticking metronome or a clapping teacher is providing aural representations of numbers: the child is hearing 3 or 4. It is quite possible that music enhances mathematical understanding by adding sound to the ways children understand numbers.

The most obvious connection is counting. Children learn rhythm by counting. Although the beat of music is in some ways an abstraction, it is very concrete when a child hears and feels it while playing. Counting while playing also presents relationships between numbers that the child may not be able to verbalize but will nevertheless understand. For example, a child has been counting four beats to a measure. A few bars later, quarter notes are replaced by eighth notes, and the teacher may suggest that the child count "one and two and three and four and" or count to eight in each measure. In the first case, the child will get a glimmer of dividing things into halves; in the second, he or she will notice, at some level, that eight is twice as many as four.

The notes themselves introduce the concept of fractions. In 4/4 time, a whole note is worth four beats, a half note two, a quarter note one, an eighth note half of a beat, and so forth. Even children who have not been formally taught fractions begin to grasp these relationships. They also learn a much more abstract concept—one that in mathematics doesn't show up until algebra. If the piece is in 3/4 time, a measure is three beats, and a quarter note is worth one beat. But if the piece is in 6/8 time, there are six beats to a measure, and the eighth note is worth one. The quarter note is now worth two. In other words, students are dealing with symbols (the notes) that represent variable values. This is a fairly advanced mathematical concept, yet children learning to play an instrument grasp it readily.

Music students also easily learn the concept of grouping numbers. Each measure has a fixed number of beats, but they may be divided differently. In 4/4 time, for example, a student may play one measure with four quarter notes, then a measure with eight eighth notes, then another measure that mixes quarter and eighth notes, and then perhaps a measure with eighth notes arranged in triplets, where three eighth notes rather than two equal a beat. Although the student may not be consciously thinking about it, she is learning that one of something is equivalent to two of something else and three of something else again. And to play these different rhythms, she must group the notes in the same way that she will later learn to group numbers. Again, the abstraction is reinforced by the aural experience of hearing the music, the visual experience of seeing the notes on paper, and the tactile experience of feeling the relationships among the notes in one's fingers. Musician Arnold Steinhardt tells how his violin teacher explained this: "Learning different rhythms, for example—the concept of dividing a unit of time in two, three, or four parts (quarter, eighth, triplet, and sixteenth notes)—was difficult for me as a seven-year-old, but Moldrem simply told me to think pear, apple, pineapple, watermelon."

Looking at a page of music shows other ways that music reinforces mathematical sensibilities. A staff has five lines with four spaces between them and, if you choose to visualize it that way, a space below and a space above. The notes are arranged horizontally and vertically. For example, a chord may be written as three notes, one on top of the other, all on lines. Another chord will also be written vertically, but one of the notes will be in a space, while the others are on lines. This is a geometric representation of a spatial relationship on the keyboard and a harmonic relationship among the notes that you can hear. A scale is a series of notes traveling horizontally across the page, alternating lines and spaces: another geometric representation of a physical space on strings or keyboard and of relationships among sounds heard serially. All written music provides an abstraction in print of relationships among physical objects (keys, strings, or patterns of open and covered holes) and sounds.

Even more amazing is that each note shows several variables: duration (one beat, two beats, etc.), pitch, and (with the help of words or symbols on the page), volume. The beat is the most obviously mathematical, but pitch also has a mathematical aspect. Each note in a scale is within either a whole step or a half step of its neighbors, and melodies are made up of intervals in which the notes are played sequentially rather than simultaneously: thirds, fifths, octaves, and so on. In the case of chords, we see the intervals vertically on the page and horizontally (but concurrently) on the keyboard. In melodies, we see the distances between notes horizontally on the page: we travel from line to line, skipping a space, to get from C to E, and from line to space, skipping a space and a line, to get from C to F, and so forth.

On the keyboard, these mathematical relationships are felt in our hands—by how much space or how many fingers are between the notes. And we hear the distance, whether we are hearing a chord or a sequence of notes. On string instruments, there is a certain amount of "space" between strings, in the sense that a C string is a fifth below the G string. The young cellist knows that, by shortening the C string as he presses with his fingers, he can play D, E, and F on it. This is understood simultaneously as pitch, physical distance (between one's fingers on the string), and numerical difference (again, represented by the notes on the staff and the student's mental visualization).

Stewart Gordon has observed, more generally, that "music study reaches virtuoso heights in the realm of abstract thinking. . . . Such skills sharply developed by music study can be transferred to other areas. It is certainly no wonder that traditional associations exist between music and mathematics, music and philosophy, music and computer science (to name but a few), for these links are born to a great degree from a common utilization of and demand for abstract thinking."

We are not suggesting that music should be used to teach math. Music lessons should be used to teach music. But it is obvious that music lessons can develop students' mathematical sensibilities, subliminally introduce mathematical concepts at both concrete and abstract levels, and reinforce the mathematics that students are learning in school by providing tactile and aural representations of numbers and mathematical relationships. It's not the main point, but it can't hurt.

Emotional Intelligence

Young children experience a wide range of emotions, as any parent knows. It is important for them to recognize their emotions, express them, and learn to talk about them. As an expressive activity, music can help children with all of these goals. Listening to music provides one approach. When a piece of music conveys a very powerful mood, children will experience it as sad, happy, scary, exciting, and so forth. In talking about the music, children can learn the vocabulary of emotions as well as begin to understand that feelings are something that everyone has, and that when you say you feel happy, other people know what you mean. For example, a parent and a child might initially listen to *Peter and the Wolf* to talk about the moods of the various parts, as well as the animals, long before the child could really know what an oboe, bassoon, or clarinet might be. The duck swims calmly in the water until the wolf comes along; the march at the end shows everyone feeling very proud.

Playing music can contribute to this kind of emotional learning in a more profound way. By actively expressing a mood, their own playing allows children first to identify and name an emotion and second to express it nonverbally, communicating it to others through a new and powerful medium. Teachers often use the vocabulary of emotion to teach children musical concepts and to encourage children to play more musically and expressively. The difference between major and minor, for example, is easily understood as the difference between happy and sad, although children don't always hear that as clearly as you might expect. At his first piano lesson, for example, five-year-old A. J. was asked to name the melody his teacher had played for him. He immediately recognized "Twinkle, Twinkle, Little Star." Then the teacher played the same melody again but in minor mode. "What song is this?" asked the teacher. "'Twinkle, Twinkle' again," he said. "Does it sound the same?" "No." "What is different?" A. J. was trying hard to verbalize the difference. Suddenly his eyes lit up, his arm flew up in the air, and he cried out, "I know!!! This one is in Spanish!"

A teacher may also suggest that a child make a piece sound "happier" to encourage a brighter sound and a lighter touch. Another approach that teachers sometimes use is to suggest that the child make up a story about what is "happening" in a piece of music. The child's story may bear absolutely no relation to what the composer had in mind or the title of the piece, but if it is at all appropriate to the music, it will help the performer convey the correct mood and spirit. Yet another approach, for the child who thinks visually rather than verbally, is to imagine pictures that go with the music.

Older children need little help with the vocabulary of emotion. Indeed, teenagers often have lists of emotions at their fingertips, with very fine shades of meaning. But they almost always need ways to express and work through their often confused feelings. Music allows them to express emotions without embarrassment and without having to verbalize the ways they feel. Arnold Steinhardt has recalled, "How delicious to pour my undefined but powerful adolescent feelings into a gypsy melody or a Spanish Habanera!" In fact, practicing may be an opportunity to release a day's frustration and confusion—as well as a way to improve musical performance. (And listening to the practice session may be an opportunity for parents to glean some understanding of their child's mood as well.)

As children enter adolescence, they develop musical tastes that their parents may not share. Those of us who did not grow up with rap or heavy metal may have difficulty figuring out what the attraction is. If you cannot tolerate your child's favorite music, headphones make a great gift. At the same time, though, teenagers' tastes in classical music may change, with Romantic composers taking front and center. Drama, fire, melancholy, and other complex and extreme emotions emerge more readily when playing Chopin or Beethoven than when playing Haydn. These are important musical opportunities as well as emotional outlets. The fact that a young musician senses the emotional content of the music is a sign of musical development and sensibility. The teacher has an opportunity to expand the repertoire in ways that the student will welcome.

The emotional benefits of musical education are available to all students, regardless of talent or even dedication. Expressivity without technique will not win competitions, but it will still make playing a valuable and even therapeutic experience. Charles Cooke, a reporter and amateur pianist, has written on this point: "Practicing, whether of Sight Reading, Technique, or Repertoire, is a pleasure when one is in good spirits. And it goes deeper than pleasure when one is in low spirits, for it occupies the mind and forces worries into the background; it gives one a tonic sense of achievement; and it often lifts the bad mood entirely. Countless times I have ended in good spirits a practice session that I began in low spirits. 'In music,' wrote Carreño, 'as in all work passionately, devotedly pursued, there is a comfort like the touch of angels' wings.'"

It is not unusual for someone who has not played an instrument for some time to return to it for comfort in times of stress or unhappiness. And anyone who has developed an appreciation of music knows how listening can enhance, modify, or even totally shift one's mood.

In conclusion, music lessons can make children better learners, enhance poise and confidence, facilitate interactions with adults, and help them understand and express their feelings. Can music lessons also make your child smarter? Well, maybe. But who cares? The other benefits are so enormous that any gains on IQ tests are just sprinkles on the icing on the cake.

chapter 3:

THE BEST TIME TO BEGIN

Does the word child *necessarily have*
to be in front of prodigy?
—**Noah Adams,** *Piano Lessons*

Children become interested in music at a very young age if they hear it frequently. A toddler who can stand up and barely walk will bop in time to music with a strong beat. Two- and three-year-olds will recognize familiar songs and may hum or sing along. This does not mean that they are ready to play the violin, but it does mean that they can be encouraged to develop their musical sense and interests. Instead of always listening to music passively, they can begin to listen actively. That is, sometimes music can be the foreground activity rather than the background. Parents can put on a tape, CD, or the radio and join their children in clapping, banging a metal pie pan with a wooden spoon, ringing a bell, or engaging in some other noisy, rhythmic action. Children can march or dance, and they can sing along, even to music that does not have words. They can make up nonsense syllables and words that will help with language development as well.

Musical toys can encourage musical development too. Bells, drums, blocks with different pitches, toy xylophones—there are endless variants. Choose toys that make sounds mechanically rather than electronically. With mechanical toys, the child's physical motions affect volume and tone, which is not true for electronic or computerized toys.

Musical activity—whether singing, dancing, or banging—should be fun. It should integrate music into games and pastimes that children enjoy, making it part of their everyday lives. For example, just as hearing a story is part of your child's bedtime routine, hearing a favorite song can also make going to sleep more pleasant. Gradually, these activities can become developmental, with children clapping or banging out a greater variety of rhythms and eventually more complex rhythms, playing tunes on the xylophone instead of random notes, and so on. According to pianist Alfred Brendel, the best musical training is "to have music at home, to grow up with it."

Your child's interest in musical activities becomes one element in evaluating readiness for lessons. One student, for example, played bells at her Montessori school. As a five-year-old, she played some little tunes for her mother, who then showed her how to play them on the piano. Her mother explained that she could match the sound of each bell by playing a certain key on the piano, and the child began to spend more time at the keyboard. Both her interest and her coordination suggested that she might enjoy piano lessons.

Children should begin their engagement with music at the earliest possible age, but that does not mean that they need to start individual music lessons at age three or four. Parents are often influenced by tales of precocity among the most successful musicians: Jascha Heifetz and David Oistrakh began playing the violin before they were four years old; Yo-Yo Ma began cello lessons at four; Van Cliburn and Alicia de Larrocha began playing the piano at three! In all likelihood, their early starts were not responsible for their later success. Rather, their extraordinary aptitude led them to music at such early ages. Certainly, if your toddler begins playing an instrument while still in diapers, you should be impressed and give the child an opportunity to learn. But pressuring a very young child into music lessons will not generate interest or talent.

For prekindergarten students, group classes with lots of physical activity may be better than individual instrumental lessons. Look for eurythmics or dance classes, activities with percussion instruments, singing, or other musical experiences for small children. The availability of such instruction might be one important consideration in choosing a preschool, or you might talk to a preschool administrator about enhancing musical activity in the curriculum. Alternatively, look for a weekend program at a local college or community center. All of these activities help children prepare for instrumental lessons, enhance their enjoyment of music, and give you a better idea of their readiness for private lessons.

Prerequisites

Teachers agree that there is no ideal age for children to start music lessons. Some should begin at three, while others should wait until they are seven or eight, and yet others fall somewhere in between. Some students begin in their teens—or in their forties. Stephane Grappelli, the jazz violinist, began playing the violin when he was twelve and learned by ear. He did not learn to read music until he was fifteen. Jean-Pierre Rampal had his first flute lesson at thirteen. Far more important than age as a determining factor are the child's abilities to perform certain basic tasks.

Some of these tasks are quite straightforward. Can your child sit still for ten or twenty minutes at a time? If not, practicing is impossible and lessons will be a trial. Although most music lessons last half an hour, some teachers offer shorter lessons for younger children or include some more physically active elements in the lesson. A wiggly child needs a teacher who can direct fidgeting into productive learning. Does your child know how to listen to a teacher, pay attention, and follow directions? A preschool teacher can help you to evaluate this ability if you are not sure. Is your child comfortable with adults other than family members? It is hard to play an instrument when you are using both hands to grip your mother's arm or are hiding behind her. Can your child perform one motion with one hand and another motion with the other hand simultaneously? This is essential for beginning most instruments and for making any progress.

Children also need to have mastered some cognitive skills. They must be able to distinguish left from right, even if this takes a little thought. Music teachers are always telling children to do something with the left or the right hand, although string teachers may call them the "violin hand" and the "bow hand" with younger children. Other essential concepts are up and down (the notes on the staff move left to right and climb up and down), high and low (for pitch), short and long (for rhythm), loud and soft (for volume), fast and slow (for tempo), and—for piano— black and white. Children do not need to understand these distinctions in musical terms before they begin. For example, if they know high and low in spatial terms, they can learn the musical meaning. But if they have no concept of these terms, they will have no framework to understand pitch and no vocabulary to express it. They should be able to count to ten and should know letters and colors (some teaching systems use colors to help young children understand more complex musical ideas).

Children must be responsible enough to take care of their instruments, which are both valuable and fragile. Does your child know how to handle breakable objects with care? Can she or he be trusted not to lose a violin or leave it where it might be stepped on or sat on? Pianos are sturdier, but they do not respond well to spilled drinks or other abuse. Parents will need to teach children these attitudes and skills and reinforce them. The effort will pay off in more careful treatment of other fragile items, too.

Some instruments require specific physical attributes and abilities. The child who wants to play the tuba or double bass may have to settle for something smaller for a few years. This may turn out well: Yo-Yo Ma has remembered: "Before I began to play the cello, I saw a double bass, but since it was too big for me I had to settle for second best." (String instruments are available in scaled-down versions for smaller children, but there are limits.) Brass and woodwind instruments require that children be able to control their breathing; woodwind players (except flutists) must cope with reeds. A teacher may tell you that he or she does not accept students under a certain age because that particular instrument requires a degree of strength, size, or coordination that younger children often do not have. Alternatively, that teacher may prefer to teach older children. Check with one or two other teachers before postponing lessons. Chapter 4 discusses the advantages and disadvantages of various instruments for young children.

If your child wants to play an instrument that is accessible only to older children, consider beginning instead with the piano, which can be started when children are young. Playing the piano teaches children to read music in two different clefs, develops coordination, and gives children an opportunity to hear proper intonation and harmony. No matter what instrument your child chooses eventually, any serious musical study at the college level will require some degree of facility on the piano.

Children do not need to know how to read to begin music lessons. They can progress well without reading for quite a while. Some parents worry that trying to learn to read words in school and music at lessons will confuse children, but there is no evidence of this. In fact, there is some evidence that music lessons help children to read phonetically, because they become better at distinguishing sounds. Young children are eager to learn and can absorb a great deal. It seems far more likely that music lessons will further motivate a child to read, improve concentration, and reinforce reading skills. Children want to be able to decipher the titles (and sometimes lyrics) of the songs they play, as well as all the other text in their music books.

If your child has all of these basic skills, be sure that he or she is really interested in music lessons, and that you are too. Can both child and parents make the time commitment? One parent will have to take the child to a lesson once a week, and parents will have to supervise daily practicing. This may not seem like much time, but take a good look at your typical family schedule. If you all get up early, your child spends eight or more hours in preschool or day care, and you are just finishing the dinner dishes at seven, do you have the time and energy for music practice? There is no point in trying to get a tired, crabby child to practice. In fact, it is counterproductive, because music will become a source of conflict and anxiety rather than pleasure. It would be much better to spend the evening listening to music and to postpone lessons until your child can stay up a bit later or practice more independently. Do not overemphasize the difficulties though. If you and your child are enthusiastic about music lessons, you will probably find the time and patience. Music lessons and practicing will then become opportunities to enjoy each other's company and have fun together.

One thing you need not evaluate is your child's musical "talent," whatever that may be. Extraordinary talent will be evident at an early age, but children with average and less-than-average degrees of musical ability can also enjoy and benefit from music lessons. If your child is at all interested in music, don't worry about talent. It really isn't relevant for quite a few years.

As you evaluate your child's readiness for music lessons, try to be objective and honest. Above all, do not push your child into lessons before he or she is ready. There is no long-term advantage in starting music lessons at three rather than five or six. Indeed, if your child is not ready to sit still, work hard, and learn, lessons will be unproductive and frustrating, and you and your child will probably give up on them. One friend was a precocious child who had skipped grades, done everything ahead of schedule, and entered Harvard at the age of fifteen. At his twenty-fifth reunion, he told of waking up on his fortieth birthday and realizing that all of the speeding through childhood really didn't matter: when you're forty, you're forty. Let your child develop at the appropriate pace, and don't worry about being the first on your block to start music lessons.

Older Children

Some children do not develop an interest in music until middle school or high school. The inspiration may come from singing in the school choir, wanting to join the band or orchestra, hearing a younger brother or sister play, or feeling a need to express emotion. The adolescent years are certainly not too late to begin music lessons. Teenagers begin with cognitive and physical skills that enable them to progress more quickly than younger children. They can read, they understand fractions, their hands are bigger, and their small muscle coordination is better. They can learn to read music much more quickly than younger children. If they have decided on their own that they want to study music, they will be well motivated.

The main problem for teenaged beginners is one of ego: it can be humiliating to play elementary pieces or to see a much younger child play far more advanced music. (This can also be a strong motivation to practice hard and progress quickly, however.) These problems can be avoided, or at least reduced, and in any case they are temporary. A teacher who is sensitive to the needs of older children will choose music suited to both their age and their skills. A thirteen-year-old need not begin with "Twinkle, Twinkle, Little Star." Some teachers use simplified versions of popular songs or show tunes. Most teachers will also excuse teenagers from class recitals until they are sufficiently accomplished that public performance is not embarrassing. Teenagers who are committed to their instruments are in a position to practice longer and more effectively than younger children, and they can move quickly into more advanced pieces. A late start can also be a jump start. For example, Aram Khatchaturian began studying music at the age of twenty-one, when he left the army at the end of World War II, and eventually became a world-famous composer.

With teenagers, the parents' main job is to provide the encouragement their teens need to get through the months of being "behind." Parents can help them find the time to practice and provide whatever emotional support they need. If your teenager is really working hard, and both he and the teacher think he would benefit from longer or more frequent lessons, then try to make this possible.

Children with Special Needs

The ability to enjoy music is not limited to the musically gifted, the intellectually advanced, or the physically talented. Everyone can enjoy music, and everyone can participate in it at his or her unique level. Some physical disabilities may limit the instruments a child can play or make advanced performance difficult, but there is probably no disability that puts listening and some degree of participation outside a child's grasp. Deaf children can feel bass notes and develop an excellent sense of rhythm, blind children can learn to play by ear or read Braille music, and children with learning disabilities can be taught with adaptive strategies.

Children who physically cannot play an instrument (perhaps because of paralysis or missing limbs) can learn to listen more appreciatively and usually to sing.

The key to helping a child with disabilities to learn music is to find a teacher who knows how to work with your child or who is willing to learn. This requires that parents be very clear in explaining exactly what their child can and cannot do, and what teachers, doctors, and therapists have recommended. Honesty and clarity are particularly important for "invisible" disabilities, such as learning or emotional problems. A music teacher should not be expected to intuit or diagnose dyslexia, attention deficit disorder, or depression.

Parents may fear that a teacher will not be willing to work with their child if they disclose these problems. In fact, some teachers will not, and you need to find this out as quickly as possible. Rather than try to hide the problem, parents should be totally open and find a teacher who can deal with the child's special needs. All parents want to protect their children from rejection. Finding a teacher who understands and accepts your child will make music lessons a positive part of your child's life rather than an experience fraught with anxiety.

Sometimes special needs are temporary. A child may be having difficulty at school that interferes with concentration or practice time. Divorce, a parent's or grandparent's illness, or other difficulty in the family may also affect a child's ability to work on music. You need not share intimate details with your child's teacher, but do let him or her know when there are problems.

The first step, though, is to find the right instrument. Chapter 4 explains the advantages and disadvantages of various instruments, and how to select the best one for your child.

chapter 4:

CHOOSING AN INSTRUMENT, OR TWO

The moment I put the flute to my lips,
I felt "this is it!"

—Paula Robison, *Talking with Flutists*

Some children fall in love with a specific instrument. Gregor Piatigorsky and Mstislav Rostropovich recall astonishingly similar youthful encounters with the cello. Piatigorsky first saw and heard the cello at a symphony concert. "From that night on, armed with two sticks, a long one for the cello and a short one for the bow, I pretended to play the cello." Rostropovich began piano lessons at four, but two years later "he took a broom and a stick and tried to play them cello fashion"— probably in imitation of his cellist father. Attraction to an instrument may be extreme: one eight-year-old who had been playing the piano for three years heard a violin for the first time and told his parents, "If you don't buy me a violin I'm going to burn the piano." And when four-year-old Artur Rubinstein's parents gave him a violin to lure him away from the piano, he broke the violin in half. Robert Casadesus broke his violin, a gift from his uncle, when he was three and a half: "I didn't want to play the violin. I wanted to play the piano." Sometimes this interest develops from seeing a parent, professional musician, or other child play, and other times children are simply drawn to the sound and look of an instrument. Yet other children learn to play an instrument because that is what happens to be in the house, or because that is what the school has on hand or needs in the band.

There are many ways to introduce your child to a variety of instruments. A live performance is best—anything from a symphony concert to a performance by the high school band. Concerts by smaller ensembles give a better sense of how the individual instruments sound. An audio or video presentation of Benjamin Britten's *Young Person's Guide to the Orchestra,* Sergei Prokofiev's *Peter and the Wolf,* or Camille Saint-Saëns's *Carnival of the Animals* also brings out the sounds of specific instruments. Once your child narrows down the choices, recitals and competitions let you and your child hear what the instruments sound like at a level closer to what you can expect at home. Recordings of solos by various instruments may also help with a decision.

If your child has a special affinity for one instrument, and if there are no obstacles to playing it (such as age or size), then it's probably a good idea to follow the child's instinct. However, if your child is interested in music but not in a specific instrument, you can take a more rational approach to the decision. In this chapter we discuss the advantages and disadvantages of various instruments in terms of their appropriateness for young children, their special requirements, the kinds of music each instrument is suited for, and other issues.

Piano and Keyboard Instruments

The piano, organ, harp, and the electric keyboard and synthesizer are possibilities for many children.

Piano

Most children who begin music lessons as preschoolers start with the piano or violin. Young children with small hands can handle either instrument as beginners (violins and cellos come in reduced sizes). The popularity of the piano for students of all ages is easy to understand: it sounds good from the beginning. So long as a piano is in tune, a student may play a wrong note, but at least it will be a note and not a squeak or a quack. The piano is also versatile, used in classical, jazz, pop, and folk music. Although the modern piano did not exist in the early centuries, music for its predecessors (including the harpsichord, hammerklavier, and fortepiano) has been adapted for the piano, so that the stylistic range of classical piano music is vast. The piano is also a sociable instrument: if someone plays well-known songs at a party, singers will soon flock around. Amateur pianist Charles Cooke has noted, "The better you play, the more your circle of friends will expand. You can count on this as confidently as you can count on the sun rising."

There are also sound musical reasons for learning the piano as a first or second instrument. Pianists must learn to read two clefs (bass and treble), to recognize and assemble intervals and chords, and to hear and express more than one voice in polyphonic music. Thus, they must master a greater variety of musical concepts and automatically learn more theory. Advanced string players learn to play more than one note at a time (guitar players earlier than others), but wind and brass players cannot. Voice students are usually encouraged to study piano, and studying music at the college level requires some degree of proficiency at the keyboard. A student interested in composing music will also need to study piano. In European and American conservatories, the piano is required as a second instrument for singers and those who play other instruments.

The piano repertoire is enormous, and professional classical pianists can contemplate careers in chamber groups, with orchestras, or as soloists. There is also a large repertoire of duets for two pianos and for piano and other instruments, as well as solo pieces with piano accompaniment. Jazz pianists play as soloists and with a variety of instrumental and voice groups. Choirs and choruses of all descriptions have piano accompanists, too. School music and choir teachers must be able to play the piano. Because the piano is so popular, all but the smallest communities will have several teachers.

The piano does have some disadvantages, however. If you do not already own one, a piano is a large investment. Parents need not begin with a Steinway grand, but even a good used upright is expensive. (And unless you are knowledgeable about pianos, you will need help in evaluating the quality of a new or used instrument.) You can rent a piano until you are sure enough of your child's interest to make a large investment. Electronic keyboards are not an adequate substitute, because they do not duplicate the touch of a piano keyboard. A student trained on a real piano can always play a keyboard, but the reverse is not true. Another disadvantage is that bands and high school orchestras rarely use student pianists, and the choir teacher usually doubles as accompanist. The piano therefore is not a good choice for the student who wants to play in school ensembles. However, many jazz and rock groups include a piano or an electronic keyboard.

Organ

Organists usually begin as pianists. They need to be able to read three clefs (there is a line of music for the left hand, one for the right hand, and one for the feet), and they need to be sufficiently coordinated to play with both hands and feet. In addition, hands have to manage not only the keyboards but also the stops. Few homes have organs; they are expensive and take up space. Often, organ students must arrange to practice in a nearby church. The organ teacher is usually whoever plays the nearest organ, unless there is a music school nearby.

But there is a great deal of wonderful organ music, both solo and orchestral, and large churches have professional organists (who sometimes double as choir leaders). Playing the organ can be great fun, because you command the sounds of an entire orchestra and can get an extraordinary amount of sound out of the instrument. The organ is not a frequent choice of children, but it should not be overlooked.

Harpsichord

The harpsichord is a lovely instrument to look at and to play. Most have two keyboards, and striking the keys results in strings being plucked rather than struck, as they are on a piano. Although some music is now being written for the harpsichord, most music for the instrument was written before the nineteenth century. Most harpsichordists begin their training on the piano and then move to the harpsichord because of an interest in early music or the baroque harpsichord repertoire. It is not an instrument that typically attracts children, but adult students who have some piano background and who like early music may wish to learn it. Some students, in fact, become sufficiently interested to build their own instruments; kits are available but expensive. Harpsichord teachers are hard to find, however, unless you live near a college or university with a music school.

Harp

The harp is a beautiful, graceful instrument that is hard to play and hard to carry around. There is only one of them in most orchestras, and they don't play in every performance. They are not part of any standard chamber ensemble, and there is virtually no solo repertoire. Except for symphony orchestras, you rarely see harps played apart from weddings and other social occasions. They are supposed to have a soothing effect. Because the instrument is so physically beautiful, children sometimes express an interest in playing it, and scaled-down versions are available for younger children. The harp also has pedals, which require an added degree of coordination. Harp players must develop a good deal of strength (as well as calluses on their fingers). Children's fantasies about playing the harp seldom survive the realities. Occasionally, though, playing the harp at school will develop into a real interest in the instrument.

Electronic Keyboard and Synthesizer

Although electronic keyboards are not a substitute for the piano, some children and teenagers may want to play in a group that needs such an instrument. Keyboards cannot produce the nuances of tone that even young students can create on a real piano. Nevertheless, learning the keyboard properly teaches students to read music and to understand rhythm and harmony. They are also useful for getting young people interested in composing.

Some children may not wish to learn an instrument but may wish to experiment with music and to compose. Indeed, some children who do play an instrument may wish to work on composition for other instruments. Computer programs and synthesizers allow them to do this. For serious composing, students will need to study theory, orchestration, music history, and other subjects. But the computer may attract young people for whom the appeal of math and machines is strong, making it possible to develop their interest in music.

String Instruments

Violin, guitar, viola, cello, and double bass are popular with children of different ages and with a variety of musical tastes. String players produce sound by drawing a bow across strings or by plucking them.

Violin

The second most popular instrument for young children is the violin, probably because of its small size, the prevalence of the Suzuki method for teaching beginners, encouragement by school music teachers, and the large number of violinists that every orchestra requires. It is a difficult instrument for beginners because they must master many new skills.

However, once the initial difficulties are past, the violin is a marvelous instrument. Like the piano, it has a vast classical repertoire for orchestra, chamber, and solo performance that ranges from the medieval to the contemporary. There are a few jazz violinists and many bluegrass, Celtic, and country fiddlers. Violinists can play in school orchestras, although competition for seats can be stiff. Violins are easy to carry around, and they come in a huge range of quality and prices. Scaled-down violins can easily be rented until your child is ready for a full-size one. Learning to tune and play the instrument requires that students develop a good ear. Because the instrument is so popular, most communities have several violin teachers. Parents should make a special effort to find teachers who enjoy teaching young students.

Guitar

Although guitars are not a good choice for preschool children (whose arms are too short and hands too small), they are great for elementary school and older children. They are especially popular with teenaged boys. Because the guitar is plucked rather than bowed, the beginner cannot produce scrapes, squeaks, and squawks. Intonation may also be less of a problem because the neck of the guitar has frets to guide fingers. Mistakes are generally less grating, because the guitar (unless amplified) is quieter than bowed instruments. Like the violin, the guitar is an ancient instrument (if you count its many predecessors), and music is available from all eras. Students can play classical, Spanish, jazz, folk, or rock music on the guitar, and guitarists are popular accompanists for singers.

Guitars come in a wide range of qualities and prices, and used guitars are frequently available. The ready availability of used instruments should serve as a warning, however: a lot of people start to learn the guitar but soon give up. This is not because of any intrinsic fault in the instrument. Rather, it is because people underestimate the difficulty of learning the guitar. They may think that you can teach yourself a few chords and be the hit of the party, or at least start a rock group. But the guitar is difficult to play at all, let alone well. Students who are serious about the guitar and take lessons are as likely to continue and succeed as students of other instruments.

Guitars can be either acoustic or electric. It is musically advisable (and easier on parents and neighbors) to begin with an acoustic guitar. However, if you have a teenager who desperately wants to play the electric guitar in a rock band, you might as well give in—but not without setting some ground rules for volume and for hours of practice. Guitarists play in rock and some jazz bands and with other vocal groups, but there are no guitars in school bands or orchestras. Some chamber music includes guitars, and there is a solo guitar repertoire.

Viola, Cello, and Double Bass

The violin's larger relatives are less frequent choices for children, but they should probably be more popular than they are, at least for children who are big enough to play them. (Again, scaled-down versions are available.) Indeed, many violinists learn the viola as a second instrument, and some professional string players alternate between the two instruments.

The viola is slightly larger and lower pitched than the violin, but it is played in the same position (under the chin). One advantage of the viola is that it is less popular than the violin, so school and community orchestras are more likely to need viola players. String quartets include violas, though piano trios (violin, cello, and piano) do not. The viola has a more mellow sound than the violin because it is lower pitched, so it doesn't sound quite so awful in the hands of beginners. However, the viola does not have a very large solo repertoire—far smaller than that of the violin and smaller even than that of the cello. The viola is almost entirely a classical instrument, although there are some bluegrass violists. Although the viola is less popular, teachers are available because many violin teachers can also teach viola. For advanced study, however, students will need to find a professional violist.

The cello is larger than the viola and still lower pitched. It has a beautiful mellow sound. It is held vertically, with a peg stuck in the floor and the knees supporting it on either side. Orchestras, trios, and quartets all need cellos, and the cello has a respectable solo repertoire as well. Cello music, too, ranges over the entire history of music, including transcriptions of music originally written for earlier versions of the instrument.

The main disadvantage of the cello is its size. It is awkward to carry around (especially for small children), you can't carry it securely on your bicycle (though kids try to do this), and it needs its own seat on airplanes (unless you're willing to risk flying it as luggage). Cello teachers are somewhat harder to find than violin teachers, but a good-size community will have a few.

The largest of the string instruments is the double bass. Although a short person can play the bass by sitting on a high stool, the bass player must have large hands and long arms. The bass is part of every orchestra, but it is used very rarely in chamber music and has almost no classical solo repertoire. It is a popular jazz instrument, though. The bass is difficult to transport; a small car may not be adequate. And, because of its size, it is an expensive instrument.

Voice

We do not often think of the voice as an instrument, but it is. "Playing" it properly requires lessons and practice. The voice has certain obvious advantages over other instruments: it is free, and it is easy to carry around. The voice (in any register) has a vast choral and solo repertoire dating back to ancient times. Singers can perform classical, gospel, jazz, folk, rock, bluegrass, country, and popular music. If they can also dance and act, they can become stars of stage, screen, and television. They can join a variety of ensembles, and they can accompany themselves on the piano or sing with a professional accompanist.

Developing the voice as an instrument does require lessons, however, and it requires that the voice have potential. Not all musicians have pleasing voices or even the ability to carry a tune. Good voices can be ruined by abuse or poor teaching, too. Young children should be encouraged to sing, and if they enjoy singing and seem to have talent, parents can begin to explore the possibility of lessons. Age is especially important for vocalists. Children's voices change as they mature (girls' as well as boys'), and formal voice training is best postponed until adolescence. For younger children, ear training, theory, and piano lessons—as well as lots of choral singing—are best. If your child also has an aptitude for dancing or acting, those talents can be developed, too, at an early age.

Woodwind Instruments

Most teachers of wind instruments will not take students younger than seven or eight. Like the piano and string instruments, wind instruments require hand coordination and agility. In addition, though, wind instruments cannot be scaled down to accommodate small hands. Even more important, they require that students be able to control their breathing and shape their mouths, jaws, tongues, and teeth into the embouchure (mouth formation) necessary for each instrument. If you have ever watched a four-year-old eat spaghetti, you have a good sense of why teachers insist on waiting.

Wind instruments fall into three categories: those without reeds (flute, piccolo, and recorder), the reed instruments (clarinet and saxophone), and the double-reed instruments (oboe, English horn, and bassoon).

Flute and Piccolo

The flute is a popular and versatile instrument. You can play the flute in a band or orchestra, and it has a solid and varied solo repertoire. The chamber music repertoire has been enhanced by transcribing violin parts for flute. The flute is an old instrument, so the range of the repertoire is extensive. There are classical, Celtic, and jazz flutists. Students can start flute lessons at a slightly younger age than they can begin other wind instruments, especially if they begin with an adapted mouthpiece. The absence of a reed also makes it a better choice for young students. For parents, it is nice to know that the flute sounds pretty good even when played by a beginner. One special advantage of the flute over other wind instruments is that it is easier to continue playing with braces on your teeth.

The piccolo is the flute's higher-pitched little cousin. Many flutists add the piccolo after a few years of lessons, because it makes them more useful in the band. There is not enough piccolo music of any kind to make it suitable as a student's only instrument. Flute teachers also teach piccolo. Flute teachers can be found in most towns, and instruments can be rented from schools. When it is time to buy an instrument, you will find that flutes come in a wide range of prices. Your child's teacher can help you make a choice.

Recorder

The recorder has been revived as an instrument for performance by lovers of early music, because that is the only period in which music was written for it. (The reason composers stopped writing for the recorder is that people invented flutes, clarinets, oboes, and other instruments that had greater range and variety of tone.) Available in a range of sizes, professional instruments are made of wood and are held vertically, like clarinets and oboes, but they have no reeds. They are relatively easy to play and are less expensive than reed instruments or flutes. In fact, plastic recorders for small children can be found for only a few dollars. The recorder is sometimes taught in elementary schools, using transcriptions of children's songs written specifically for this purpose.

Playing the recorder can teach a child to read notes and to play different notes by covering different holes in the instrument. It may also pique interest in other woodwinds and is good preparation for playing the flute. Its use is restricted almost entirely to early music ensembles, making it a poor choice for children.

Clarinet

Like the flute, the clarinet is popular in part because of its versatility: it is vital to bands and orchestras, it is prominent in jazz and classical music, and it has a large chamber and solo repertoire. It is about an octave lower than the flute and has a broad range (nearly three and a half octaves). Music specifically written for the clarinet dates to the early eighteenth century.

Children can begin clarinet lessons when their hands are big enough. As is true for most wind instruments, the main difficulties in learning the clarinet are the embouchure and fingering. It takes a bit longer for a clarinetist to sound good than it does a flutist, but (except for an occasional squawk) the clarinet is not too hard on parents' ears. Because of the clarinet's popularity and prominence in bands, teachers are fairly plentiful, and instruments can be rented from schools until it is time to buy one. Better clarinets are made of wood.

Saxophone

The saxophone is mainly a band and jazz instrument. It has a single reed, like the clarinet, but it is made of metal and has a very different tone. Clarinetists and flutists interested in classical music sometimes choose the saxophone as a second instrument because it makes them more useful orchestra members: on the rare occasion that a saxophone is needed, they can take over. For band or jazz musicians, the saxophone may be a good first or only instrument. Most people are attracted to the saxophone by its sound, which is hard to describe but quite haunting. Many clarinet teachers also teach saxophone.

Oboe, English Horn, and Bassoon

The double reed branch of the woodwind family includes the most difficult instruments, and they are not good choices for young beginners. Children who fall in love with the oboe or bassoon when listening to *Peter and the Wolf* should probably begin with the clarinet and move on to the oboe or bassoon later.

The difficulty of these instruments is due largely to its use of a double reed. These reeds make it more difficult to get a sound out of the instruments (any sound, let alone the right sound), and the reeds themselves are difficult to fit and maintain. In fact, professional oboists and serious amateurs usually make their own reeds. The modern oboe is a twentieth-century refinement of an instrument invented in the seventeenth century with even older roots, so the repertoire is varied. Oboes are found in all orchestras, some bands, and many chamber groups. There are many solo pieces for oboe, and it is almost exclusively a classical instrument.

The English horn is slightly larger and lower pitched than the oboe, and it has a spherical bowl at the bottom. It is an orchestral, classical instrument. Except for a few professional orchestra members, most English horn players also play the oboe.

The largest and deepest of the double reeds are the bassoons. They share the difficulties of the oboe and are even more problematic for young players because of their size. The contrabassoon, or double bassoon, is an octave lower than the bassoon and even larger. Both varieties of bassoon are orchestral, classical instruments. They are possibilities as second instruments or as first instruments for older beginners.

Qualified oboe, English horn, and bassoon teachers are difficult to find outside cities with symphony orchestras or music schools.

Brass Instruments

Brass instruments (trumpet, trombone, tuba, and French horn) are played by using one's lips as a sort of vibrating reed stretched over the mouthpiece, which varies in shape and size depending on the instrument and the performer's preference. Brass players use valves or slides to determine the pitch of the notes. Like the woodwinds, brass instruments require control of breathing and coordination of the mouth, lips, and tongue to achieve the proper embouchure. Most brass teachers recommend waiting until children are at least eight or nine to begin lessons. The larger instruments (trombone and tuba) require physical strength and arm length that most children do not acquire until a few years later. The child set on learning a brass instrument usually starts with the trumpet and may later move on to a larger instrument.

All of the brass instruments are played in bands and orchestras. Although it is difficult to achieve correct intonation, children can quickly learn to get a clear, loud sound out of their instruments and achieve a fair degree of proficiency.

Trumpet

The trumpet is the basic brass instrument, found in marching, symphonic, and dance bands, in orchestras, in classical brass ensembles, and in jazz combos. It also has a large solo repertoire in music of all periods. The trumpet is the preferred beginning brass instrument, and parents should have no difficulty in renting an instrument or finding a teacher.

Trumpets come in various sizes, which play in different registers. Once a student has learned the basics, it sounds pretty good. This is fortunate, because trumpets are loud. That may be one reason why they are so popular with young children. Along with their volume comes a bright, clear sound that most people find appealing.

Trombone

Trombone players produce sound the same way trumpet and other brass players do, but they use a slide to control intonation instead of valves. (There are also valve trombones, but slide trombones are far more common.) The trombone is larger than the trumpet and somewhat harder to play, but it is a very popular band and jazz instrument. It is not a classical solo or chamber instrument.

Tuba

The tubas (euphonium, bombardon, and others) are the largest brass instruments, and intonation is controlled by valves. They are too big and heavy for small children to manage, and they require a lot of breath. Sousaphones are large, circular tubas—the instruments that wrap around and seem to envelop their players. Tubas are found in bands, orchestras, and some chamber ensembles. They have virtually no solo repertoire and are usually not jazz instruments.

French Horn

The French horn is the most difficult of the brass instruments. It is the circular instrument that is played with the right hand inserted into the bell, where it controls tone and intonation. At concerts, you will notice French horn players emptying their spit valves frequently, a somewhat messy process that may appeal to young players. French horns are found in bands, orchestras, and chamber ensembles, and they have a large solo classical repertoire. When played well, the French horn has a somewhat muted, haunting sound that is quite lovely.

Percussion

Percussion instruments include anything that produces a sound by being struck: blocks, triangles, drums, xylophones, gongs, cymbals, chimes, and so forth. A professional percussionist must master a broad range of instruments. Because percussion provides the underlying rhythm, these instruments are found in bands, orchestras, and jazz and rock groups.

Children like percussion instruments for many reasons. They are usually encouraged to play them very early in school, so these instruments are familiar. Most percussion instruments do not have any variation in pitch (xylophones, chimes, and tympani—kettle drums—are the main exceptions), so rhythm is the only element to be learned. And most percussion instruments can be played so that they make a lot of noise. This, of course, is what makes them somewhat less popular with parents.

The downside of all of this is that most percussion instruments do not play any melody, and rhythm alone can become quite boring. When percussionists play with other instruments in a group, they become part of the music. Practicing alone, though, can be dull. Also, students can avoid learning to read music, which sooner or later works to their disadvantage.

Good percussion teachers conquer these problems by having their students learn instruments that do have pitch and by creating percussion ensembles for their students. There is no difficulty in finding percussion teachers who can make a good band player out of your child. However, a student who wants to be a professional percussionist will need to study with an orchestra member or other professional.

Choosing a Second Instrument

Children who enjoy music often decide they want to learn a second instrument. Some children, in fact, begin two instruments at once and then choose the one they like better. Piano students may decide they want to join the school band or orchestra, so they will take up the violin, flute, or something else that allows them to join an ensemble. A child who has started with the violin or cello because it was the only instrument small enough may want to move on to the double bass when that becomes possible. Sometimes exposure to more music leads children to discover that something other than what they are playing is their dream instrument. These are all good reasons to start a second instrument. The big decision is whether to add on the new instrument or to give up the first one.

In making this choice, you and your child need to think about time, money, and motivation. If it is difficult to find time to practice one instrument, it will be doubly difficult to find time to practice two. If the reason for choosing a second instrument is to play in a band or orchestra, then all of the time considerations of practicing and performing with an ensemble (discussed in chapter 8) come into play as well. And there will be two weekly lessons to attend. The cost of lessons will double, along with the cost of music. And you will need to rent or buy a second instrument, unless one is available free from your child's school. This may be quite expensive.

Finally, your child will need to stay motivated enough to keep up with both instruments. The new instrument will have the advantage of excitement and novelty, but the results will not sound as good for a while. However, the learning curve is less steep with a second instrument, because your child already knows how to count and read music. At first, the earlier instrument may suffer because something new is almost always more intriguing. Eventually, though, your child will have to find a way to balance the two interests (along with schoolwork, chores, and everything else in life).

Of course, giving up the first instrument may make sense. If it was just a stopgap until your child could move on to what he or she really wanted to play, there may be little reason to continue. If progress on the first instrument was always lackluster, and the new one spurs your child on to good work, it may be time to switch. And if the new teacher is more to your liking and seems to inspire greater dedication, that is another good reason to change.

Giving up that first instrument may not be sensible, though. Especially if you have found an excellent teacher whom you and your child both like, it may be best to continue with lessons. Certainly, if the second instrument is just a means to an end—playing in the band—and not a serious interest, then the first instrument can remain the focus of your child's efforts. In fact, your child may not want to continue private lessons on the second instrument once the basics are mastered.

It is unusual for a child (unless extraordinarily gifted) to excel at two instruments, if only because of the time involved. (Exceptions are closely related instruments like the violin and viola or clarinet and saxophone.) If your child starts a second instrument and wants to continue with the first, allow some time—at least a year—for a decision about which instrument will be the focus of effort. Include both teachers in the decision. And remember, the decision need not be final. If your child has dedicated several years of work to the piano or violin, returning after a year or two of playing the guitar or trumpet is always possible.

Harmony among Siblings

If you have more than one child, and they all want to study an instrument, should they play the same one? Should you direct your three children to the piano, violin, and cello so that they can form a trio? Perhaps parents and children can join together and form a brass quintet. Let's look at the possibilities.

Once you have invested in a piano and found a wonderful teacher, it is very tempting to stick with the piano for all your children. That may make a great deal of sense: it saves time, money, and trouble. However, it will work only if all of your children like the piano and if they are not highly competitive with one another. For example, if your oldest child is a talented pianist and an excellent student, your second or third child—no matter how talented and bright—will probably resent being compared with the eldest. In this case, the younger children should be allowed to choose different instruments. In a contrasting example, suppose that your first child has been taking lessons for some time and is making average progress. Your second child begins lessons with the same teacher and just takes off: within a year, child number two has surpassed child number one and is the star of class recitals. Unless the elder child is unusually gracious and loving, there will be little peace in your home.

This is not a musical decision, and it is one that parents are best equipped to make. If your children play happily together, share friends, and are not overly competitive, then they can probably play the same instrument. In one family, sibling rivalry was clearly not a problem. Six-year-old Anna was getting ready for her first sonatina festival. To explain what a festival or competition is, her teacher pointed to a picture of Anna's older brother receiving a gold medal in last year's festival. "Anna," she said, "if you play really, really well, you may even receive a gold medal like your brother." "I don't want a gold medal," Anna replied. "I want a silver one." "Why?" her puzzled teacher and mother asked. "Because I don't want to confuse his medal with mine." If your children fight a lot and compete over other things, then they should play different instruments—maybe even instruments in different families. When they get older and have worked out their difficulties with each other, they may be able to play duets.

If you are sure that your children should not play the same instrument, and they are beginning lessons at the same time, they may decide to make life difficult by insisting that they must both play the flute or they will die. At that point, you can give in and adjudicate the ensuing battles; you can tell them that neither one can play the flute ("Now, who wants the violin and who wants the trumpet?"); or you can get them to agree to accept the results of a coin toss. Musically, it is unlikely to matter. If two competitive siblings study the same instrument with the same teacher, they should take lessons on different days and play different music. The teacher will understand the problem and cooperate.

You may also want to think about whether your child should play the same instrument as you or your spouse. Children can feel quite competitive toward their parents, and that may become a problem. Also, if your child prefers to exclude you from practice and lessons, you may feel less rejected if your own instrument is not involved. Finally, if you tend to be overly controlling or interfering, a different instrument would be a good idea.

Time Never Wasted

Just as music comes in almost endless varieties, prospective musicians have a wealth of instruments to choose from. Making the decision about what to study can be a great deal of fun. You and your child can listen to lots of music, attend a variety of performances, and learn much about instruments and playing styles. Simply learning to identify the sounds of different instruments is an accomplishment for your child. What is important is choosing an instrument that meets your child's musical goals and finding a good teacher. The decision is not irreversible. Lessons on any instrument are a worthwhile investment, and the time spent on learning an instrument is never wasted.

chapter 5:

CHOOSING THE RIGHT TEACHER

*I knew then that my primary responsibility . . .
was not to improve his technique but to make
sure that his talent was properly nourished
by exposure to great music.*

—Mark Salzman, *The Soloist*

Just as the first kindergarten teacher or first math or language teacher may influence your child's attitude toward school and specific subjects, the first music teacher may play a decisive role in your child's musical development, his or her attitude toward music in general, and his or her relationship to the chosen instrument. A good music teacher will introduce students to the world of music with excitement and encouragement, with a contagious love for music and the instrument, and your child's first musical experience will be positive, memorable, and lasting. But a mediocre or burned-out teacher may forever destroy your child's desire to study music by transmitting indifference and boredom. So the first formal musical experience often determines whether music will become part of your child's life, and this experience depends on the quality of the first teacher.

Many parents mistakenly believe that, at the beginning stages of music education, the quality of the teacher is not important and that later, if the child "shows talent" and interest, they will find a better teacher. The great pianist Josef Lhevinne, who taught many fine performers, wrote:

> The teacher of beginners is a person of great importance in all education, particularly in music. In Russia the teacher of the beginners is often a man or a woman of real distinction. The work is not looked upon as an ignoble one, worthy of only the failures or the inferior teacher. These teachers are well paid. Of course, in America you are developing many teachers of beginners who have had real professional training for this work; but in the past there must have been some ridiculously bad teachers of elementary work, judging from a few of the so-called advanced pupils whom I have been called upon to teach. The folly of paying a teacher a considerable fee for instruction that should have been given at the very beginning is too obvious to comment upon. Surely a practical people like the Americans will rectify this.

When choosing a music teacher for a young child, parents must consider not only the teacher's professional qualifications but also his or her personality and teaching experience. A brilliant musician is not always the best teacher, and a knowledgeable college professor may not be the right fit for a young child. Unlike a short-term teacher–student relationship at school, where teachers change every year, a private music teacher may be the only adult outside the family with whom your child forms a long-term relationship, lasting not only throughout the school years but perhaps for a lifetime. The music teacher will influence your child's musical development, taste, and understanding. It is not uncommon for the music teacher to become not only an authority in the area of music but also a personal friend, counselor, and parent figure.

So how do you go about finding the right teacher for your child? If you live in a small town, you may not have many choices. You may be lucky to have one music teacher who knows a few instruments and teaches music and band in school. Sometimes this teacher may accept a few better students privately for individual lessons. However, this may not be right for your child. Find out whether there are other music teachers in neighboring towns; sometimes it is worth commuting a bit for a better musical education.

If you live in a large cultural center, you may face a different challenge: How should you choose among many highly qualified, sometimes well-known, music teachers? How can you make the right decision? Most likely your first references will come from friends and neighbors whose children take lessons. Be careful. Evaluate those who gave you the referral. Do they have any musical background? Are their goals for music education similar to your own? What do they know about the teacher? Why and how did they choose this person? Remember that music teachers are not licensed and need not be certified: anyone can hang out a shingle. More often than not, you will find that your friends chose a teacher for convenience: a woman in the neighborhood who supplements her family income by giving music lessons for a reasonable fee. Most likely, she never had formal music education but took private lessons as a child. Now those lessons are coming in handy. In today's busy world, with endless carpools and an overload of extracurricular activities, this may sound like a blessing. What could be more convenient? Your child walks to music lessons while you do some of your errands. Such a teacher may be acceptable in some cases, especially in a small town with few choices. However, if your child has above-average musical abilities or interest and your goal for music education stretches beyond learning how to play a few simple arrangements of

Christmas carols, don't be seduced by convenience and low fees. At least, do not make these issues a priority when making your final decision.

Ask around, collect a few names, call the music department of your local college or university for references, or find out whether there is a local music teachers' association and whether it has a referral service. Music stores and professional musicians may also offer suggestions. Some of the national associations listed in "For Further Information" offer referrals. Do your homework and then begin calling prospective teachers.

What should you ask? The common mistake parents make is to call a teacher, ask whether there are openings in the teacher's schedule, and immediately sign up for lessons. Most good teachers will not do this. Even if they have an opening, they will first invite you and your child for an interview. This interview is important for the teacher, the parents, and the child. While the teacher evaluates your child's musical and physical abilities, maturity level, and motivation, and explains the studio philosophy and policies, you will evaluate the teacher. This may be the first time you have seen the person to whom you are going to entrust your child for many years of weekly visits, music education, and tremendous influence.

This may also be your first chance to evaluate, at least superficially, the teacher's personality. It is appropriate to ask about the teacher's educational background, music training, teaching experience, membership in the Music Teachers National Association (MTNA), and national certification. You may also ask whether the students of this studio participate in competitions and other performances and whether the teacher holds annual or semiannual class recitals. Ask permission to observe a lesson, preferably with a student close in age to your own child, or to attend a class recital. While observing a lesson, notice the style in which the teacher talks to the student, explains new material, makes critical comments, and relates to the child. Does the lesson have a professional atmosphere? Are you comfortable with the level of formality? Is the teacher able to engage the child?

It is important for your child to observe the lesson as well. Watch your child watching the lesson! You will be able to tell fairly easily whether he or she finds the teacher engaging, responds well to the atmosphere, or feels intimidated or uncomfortable.

Do not ask the teacher to play for you; that is not appropriate. If you are interested in the teacher's performance skills, ask whether she or he plans any performances in the near future that you might attend. The performance might even be one of the class recitals. Of course, a good teacher must be able to play reasonably well. Remember, though, that performance skills are not always a good indicator of teaching skills. Far more important than performance skills is the teacher's ability to inspire students and to teach not only technique but also musicianship.

It is essential that teachers and parents be honest during the interview. If your child has any learning or other disability, tell the teacher about it at the outset and ask about experience with other children with similar conditions. If you do not disclose a problem, the teacher may have expectations about attention span and concentration that your child cannot meet. The result will be a disappointed teacher and a disheartened child. The teacher must be honest too, not only about experience with similar problems but also about willingness to take on a child with disabilities. If the teacher is interested in working with your child and has had experience with similar disabilities, it is appropriate to ask about how he or she will adapt teaching strategies to help your child.

You should also be honest about your goals and about how committed you and your child are to music lessons. Is this a tentative undertaking that you hope will work out, or is learning to play an instrument a lifelong dream? Is your child hoping for (or dreaming of) a musical career, or just to be able to play a few guitar chords at parties? Does your child dream of becoming a rock star or a classical violinist? All these goals are worthy, but not every teacher will be equally sympathetic to them. You are trying to match your child's personality, interests, and goals with the right teacher, not find a paragon who is absolutely the best for everyone.

The interview is also an opportunity for the teacher to ask you and your child some questions. You may expect the teacher to ask about your commitment to your child's music education and your goals. The teacher may also give your child a basic test, such as clapping rhythms or singing a melody. Some teachers may also look at your child's hands to evaluate physical potential.

A teacher may reject your child based on this preliminary evaluation. Does that mean the doors of the musical world are closed for your child? No! It simply means you must find another teacher or choose another instrument. Some teachers are interested only in gifted and dedicated students who want to become professional musicians, while others will accept students with average musical abilities and find ways to develop those abilities. You may even encounter a negative teacher who will tell you not to bother with music lessons at all. In this case, always seek a second opinion, or even a third. If a piano teacher rejects your child because she or he has very small hands, you may want to consider another instrument. However, you may just decide to live with the fact that your child will probably play more Haydn and Mozart than Rachmaninoff or Liszt!

Attending a class recital will give you a better general idea of the professional level of the students and the teacher. You will hear what kinds of music the students play, how well they are prepared, and how professionally the recital is organized. You can also see whether the students are comfortable in performing and how they relate to the teacher. They should be respectful but not awestruck; comfortable but not overly familiar. Above all, they should enjoy the recital—even if they make a few mistakes.

Attending a lesson and a recital will give both you and your child a good sense of what it will be like to study with the teacher. Discuss both visits with your child and make sure that your child likes the teacher and looks forward to studying with him or her. Ask your child, "Would you like to play in next year's recital?"

You also have an opportunity to assess the physical surroundings where your child will be taught. Whether it is a room in the teacher's home or a studio, the space should offer certain features. A piano teacher's instrument should be in good condition (no broken keys!) and in tune. Ideally, a piano studio should have two pianos so that student and teacher can play together, or two children can play duets. Teachers of other instruments should also have a piano available so that the young violinist or flutist can learn to play with an accompanist.

The studio should be clean and well lighted, and there should be a place for a parent to sit. In fact, it is a good idea for there to be a chair for the parent in the room and one outside, either in a hall or in a waiting room. Older children especially may prefer not to have their parents present. Also, a parent's presence may sometimes disrupt lessons if a child appeals to the parent for a second opinion or tends to show off.

Look for a good supply of music and a library of books about music and teaching. Photographs of children from recitals or competitions are also a good sign, though you shouldn't expect to see these in a teacher's living room, if that is where lessons are held. Many teachers will have a tape recorder to record pieces for children, to record students' playing, or to play professional tapes. Do not expect equipment of recording studio quality, though. A clean, convenient bathroom should also be available.

Watch out for possible distractions. If there is a telephone in the room, it should have an answering machine. If the teacher teaches at home, other residents—adults and children—should not wander into the room. Teachers with small children should have someone looking after them during lesson times. If your child will be walking or biking to lessons or taking public transportation, you need to be comfortable with the route and the neighborhood.

What should you do if you find an ideal teacher for your child but the teacher's schedule is full? Ask whether there is a waiting list and how long you may need to wait. If the waiting period is a year or longer, ask the teacher to recommend someone else who might be just as appropriate for your child. You may even ask for a few names and arrange interviews with all of them. However, if your child is still very young (under five), and if you and your child have your hearts set on this teacher, you can wait. Just continue playing music, singing, and keeping your child's interest alive.

Teaching Methods

During the interview, you may ask questions about the methods the teacher uses and programs the students participate in, such as state study programs with annual examinations. According to Josef Hofmann, a brilliant pianist who emigrated to the United States from Poland in the early twentieth century, "America is the most method-ridden country in the world." Hundreds of methods are offered, and it is impossible for a parent, especially one without any musical background, to understand the advantages and disadvantages of even a fraction of them. The bottom line is that all of these methods will, one way or another, teach your child how to read and understand music. It is up to the teacher to choose which road will lead to the best results. A good teacher is the key element. An experienced teacher is familiar with several methods and knows which works best, or has his or her own method, or combines several methods in a way that has proven successful. Before you engross yourself in studying the differences between Yamaha, Orff, Suzuki, Kodály, and other methods, find a good, experienced teacher and discuss what will work best for your child, considering your child's abilities, motivation, and objectives. Be leery of a teacher who is fanatically committed to a single teaching method.

Look for a teacher who wants to impart a love of music. Pianist Arthur Schnabel felt teachers should "try to release the creative impulse and urge in a child . . . try to make the child like what it is asked to do, as much as possible. Even if the child in the first half-year of its instruction does not learn much, technically, one should not worry." We agree. The important thing in the beginning, especially with younger children, is to create a love of music and joy in playing and listening. Look for a teacher who has an infectious love of music and takes pleasure in teaching it.

Practical Matters

Other important issues to discuss during the interview are costs and studio policies. A well-organized professional music studio will provide a written statement of rules, regulations, and fee schedules. This will include tuition and other fees (such as registration, books, competition applications, etc.) as well as policies about missed lessons, holidays, summer breaks, and other scheduling matters. Some studios or teachers require parents to sign a contract. Read it carefully, as you would any contract, and ask questions about anything that is unclear before signing it. Some studios require that tuition be paid a month in advance, while others divide it into three semesters. Some music studios have a group of teachers of different instruments working together in the same building under the same set of rules. In this case, they may have one or two people who handle the administrative matters. An individual teacher working at home may or may not have a written policy. If not, you still must discuss all issues concerning finances and rules, preferably at the interview, but certainly before the first lesson. There are no generally accepted rules and regulations for music teachers or small private studios. Tuition costs may vary from a few dollars to a hundred or more for an hour. Some teachers offer a trial period—several months during which the teacher and student get to know each other and then decide whether to continue their collaboration.

When you sign up with a studio or a teacher, you are responsible for paying tuition on time, according to the studio's schedule. Many music teachers are uncomfortable about financial matters, so show your respect and don't wait to be reminded about payments. Repeated tardiness about payments may lead a teacher to suggest that you find another teacher.

What about a teacher who comes to your home instead of teaching in a studio? This practice is common in some communities. It may sound attractive because of the convenience for busy parents. However, these lessons may resemble home tutoring rather than teaching at a high professional level. It may be acceptable in some cases (and certainly better than no lessons at all, if this is the only way you can manage), yet you may find that the quality of the teachers who are willing to teach in this way is not up to your expectations. Sometimes they are students themselves, without teaching skills or experience, who supplement their income by giving lessons. They may quit as soon as they finish school or find a better job. Others may be retired people without formal training or musicians between jobs. Many such teachers will not treat these lessons very seriously, although there are always exceptions. In addition, your child may regard lessons at home, in such a familiar setting, as something other than "real school," and discipline will suffer.

If the cost of hiring a highly professional music teacher is prohibitive, do not despair. Scholarships and other sources of financial aid are available. If your child is talented and highly motivated, you will have no problem finding financial help. You can begin by asking the school music teacher, the Boys & Girls Clubs, and the local music teachers' association. Don't hesitate to ask the private teacher about financial assistance. Music teachers are usually quite responsive to such needs and probably will be able to put you in touch with institutions, organizations, or private individuals who will be able to help. Some studios have their own scholarship programs.

Time for a Change?

It sometimes becomes necessary to change music teachers. However, this should not be done frivolously. For example, if you think that another teacher's students play better in competitions or other performances, do not rush to the phone to ask for an interview. Remember that any transition may cause a lot of problems. Adjusting to a new teacher will take time. If your child is comfortable with the current teacher, the change may even be traumatic.

If your child's teacher moves away, most likely he or she will recommend another teacher, probably with a similar background, approach, and work ethic. If not, simply start all over with the procedure described earlier for finding a teacher. It should be easier for you the second time around, because you will have a better sense of what is important to you and your child.

If you are looking for a new teacher because there is no chemistry between your child and the present teacher and the learning process is suffering, or because your child has outgrown the teacher and needs more of a challenge, make the change tactfully. Discontinue lessons with the present teacher. You might want to take a little break before looking for a new teacher unless you already have someone in mind. Most teachers will not accept students who have been working with another teacher without notifying the first teacher.

Your child's music teacher may initiate the change, too. Good teachers recognize that they cannot work well with all students, and they may suggest that parents begin to look elsewhere. They may even provide some names of teachers they feel would be better suited to a child's needs. A teacher may also suggest that your child end lessons because little progress is being made. In that case, you will need to decide whether this is because your child really has gone as far as possible (or desirable) with music or whether a new teacher will solve the problem.

Before making any change, discuss the matter with your child. A child who has invested time and effort in music lessons has developed preferences about teaching styles and personalities. If your child seems to be making little progress, the suggestion of changing teachers may provoke a variety of responses. Your child may be delighted, because she or he was uncomfortable with the teacher but afraid to say so. Or your child may be unhappy about the idea. Your child may be very fond of the teacher but has nevertheless been lazy about practicing. In this case, the mere suggestion of changing teachers may be enough to solve the problem.

chapter 6:

PRACTICING

If we do only what is required of us we are slaves;
the moment we do more we are free.

—Cicero

W e learned clichés growing up—"'How do you get to Carnegie Hall?' 'Practice!'" "Practice makes perfect."—and now we repeat them to our children. We teach them that if they want to excel in sports, ballet, music, or any other endeavors, they need to work hard and be very determined. However, more often than not, practicing a musical instrument remains the biggest challenge for students and the most frequent reason for quitting lessons.

Most children do not like to practice and are quite inventive about excuses to avoid it. When parents remind their children to practice, the response may be:

- I am thirsty (or hungry or hot or cold).
- I have a headache (or a stomachache).
- I need to go to the bathroom.
- I can't find my music.
- I have too much homework.
- The dog chewed my music.
- I need to think (followed by a long break for daydreaming).

When you hear these excuses, don't be discouraged. You are not alone. Young children do not understand the word *practice*. They want to play an instrument and have fun. Maybe instead of asking, "Did you practice today?" We should ask, "Did you play the piano (or violin, or flute) today?" Pianist Arthur Schnabel recommended that we "eliminate the term 'practice' from the vocabulary. . . . I would ask them: 'Have you already made and enjoyed music today? If not—go and make music.'" Practicing is hard; playing or making music is fun.

Can practicing be enjoyable? Yes, and it should be. Yet practicing correctly is an art in itself and should be taught from the beginning. If a child masters this art, the result will be more than rewarding. Not only will he or she master musical skills, but the time spent with the instrument can include some of life's most exciting, exhilarating, creative, and illuminating moments—not to mention numerous fringe benefits such as developing self-esteem, will power, discipline, determination, focus, attention to detail, and just the pure enjoyment of listening to or making music and being able to express oneself and one's feelings. The word *practice* should not be synonymous with the word *boredom*. Mindless repetition is boring. Intelligent, goal-oriented work is fun.

Developing Practice Skills

Practicing needs to be taught and learned. Ivan Galamian, a noted violinist and the teacher of such superstars as Itzhak Perlman and Pinchas Zukerman, believed that it is impossible to overestimate the importance of practicing: "If we analyse the development of the well-known artists, we see that in almost every case the success of their entire career was dependent upon the quality of their practicing. . . . the lesson is not all. Children do not know how to work alone. The teacher must constantly teach the child how to practise." If you become concerned about your child's progress or practice skills, talk to the teacher, attend lessons, and ask questions. Although not all lessons should be practice sessions, ask your teacher to give a lesson in practicing occasionally, and use it as a model for practicing at home.

To help students organize their practice time, teachers may suggest a practice log. This might be a simple chart with six points: (1) time started, (2) goal, (3) method of work, (4) problems, (5) time finished, and (6) result. Students use one log weekly for each piece they are working on (see opposite page).

Start and finish times are important because most young children have a poor perception of time. Very often they feel they have practiced for a "long" time, while in reality only a few minutes have passed. Noting the beginning and end of a practice session will give them a more realistic understanding of the time needed to achieve a goal and of the time they have actually spent.

Identifying a goal before beginning to practice is most important: it makes practicing purposeful rather than mindless. The goal is whatever assignment a teacher gave for each piece of music. It can be correcting mistakes, learning notes, working on dynamics, tone, expression, fingering, memorization, or any number of other things.

The method of work needs to be thought through. Often when a teacher asks, "How did you work on this piece?" the answer is, "Oh, I played it many, many times." "How many?" "I don't know. I didn't count. Maybe three."

PRACTICE LOG

*Name of Piece:*_____ *The Week of:*_____

Time Started:_____	Time Started:_____
Goal:_____	Goal:_____
_____	_____
_____	_____
Method of Work:_____	Method of Work:_____
_____	_____
Problems:_____	Problems:_____
Time Finished:_____	Time Finished:_____
Result:_____	Result:_____

Time Started:_____	Time Started:_____
Goal:_____	Goal:_____
_____	_____
_____	_____
Method of Work:_____	Method of Work:_____
_____	_____
Problems:_____	Problems:_____
Time Finished:_____	Time Finished:_____
Result:_____	Result:_____

Time Started:_____	Time Started:_____
Goal:_____	Goal:_____
_____	_____
_____	_____
Method of Work:_____	Method of Work:_____
_____	_____
Problems:_____	Problems:_____
Time Finished:_____	Time Finished:_____
Result:_____	Result:_____

Obviously, those practicing sessions were a waste of time. With the teacher's help, students should decide on the method of work needed for each piece, whether it is playing slowly, breaking a piece down into small sections and working on a particular problem, or playing it from the beginning to the end, trying to achieve unity.

Problems need to be identified before they can be corrected. If a problem persists, it needs to be understood and brought to the lesson. Students need to ask questions, and teachers need to answer them.

Asking children to write down the result of their practicing teaches them to evaluate their work and recognize problems. Sometimes the self-evaluations are quite funny, but even these provide useful information:

> Time started: 6:45
> Goal: Get the cords memorized.
> Method of work: Played it.
> Problems: Cords
> Time finished: 7:00
> Result: All cords memorized except 1. I don't get it.

The results of one day's practice may or may not be satisfactory, but the system makes students more conscientious about their work and eventually brings a lot of satisfaction. Not only do the practicing and playing improve, but the students can see how their own activities led to improvement.

If a child is taught the correct way of practicing from the beginning, parental supervision will not be necessary and the tension that usually arises in connection with practicing will be relieved. Often parents ask, "How long should he practice?" or "How many times should she play this piece?" The answer is: as long as it takes to achieve a goal. And since each student's goals are different for each piece and from week to week, different amounts of time will be needed to achieve them. Pianist Josef Hofmann gave this answer:

> Playing too much in one day has often a deteriorating effect upon one's studies, because work is profitable, after all, only if done with full mental concentration, which can be sustained only for a certain length of time. Some exhaust their power of concentration quicker than others; but however long it may have lasted, once it is exhausted all further work is like

unrolling a scroll which we have laboriously rolled up. Practise self-examination, and if you notice that your interest is waning—stop. Remember that in studying, the matter of quantity is of moment only when coupled with quality.

Practice time at home is the most important part of learning a musical instrument. Most students meet with their teachers once a week for a half-hour or hour-long session. This lesson time should be spent learning new material, making new discoveries, polishing a recital piece, or doing something else for which the teacher's presence is essential. If a student comes unprepared, with the same uncorrected mistakes, incorrect fingering, or unlearned text as the week (or two or three weeks) before, the lesson becomes boring and frustrating for both student and teacher. To avoid this problem, children need their parents' help. Parents need to express the same concern and show the same respect for the child doing music homework that they show for school homework. Children should know that music lessons are just as important for their education as math, reading, and other school subjects. Accepting this basic commitment answers many of the questions parents raise about motivating children to practice.

The Parents' Role

All successful music students have supportive families. It has been said that behind every great musician is a mother or father. This was certainly true of Mozart and Beethoven. Of course, their parents' strict methods are not appropriate for today's children and might even be considered abusive. Yet parents' enthusiasm, encouragement, and participation are still essential, especially for beginners and young children. Music teachers understand that they may not win every competition with soccer, basketball, cheerleading, or even ballet. But they also know that the gift of music will last longer than the benefits of these other activities. Remembering the ultimate goal—whether it is making your child a fine musician or ensuring that your child will have a lasting love of music—is what makes practicing worth the occasional conflict.

Even with parents' best intentions, practicing can become a battleground on which parents and children struggle for control. Violinist Arnold Steinhardt has described a rather extreme example: "Things came to a head after Mother demanded one time too many that I practice. In a child's rage, I broke the violin over the corner of our dining-room table. There we stood, facing each other, in shock over what I had done. The violin hung limply by its strings, still attached to the neck I held in my trembling hand." (His mother remembered the incident differently, claiming that it was she who had broken the violin. Either way, it was clearly a bad moment.) To avoid warfare—but get the practicing done—parents need to be sensitive to their evolving relationship with their child. When children are young, they may welcome or even need their parents' presence and help. As they grow older, and especially when they become teenagers, they may prefer to practice in solitude. Parents' participation depends in part on their children's attitude.

It also depends on their children's needs. Some children need help to sit still and focus, while others will happily practice for reasonable periods without supervision. Some need their parents to help with posture, tuning, counting, or fingering. Some need reminding about the teacher's instructions. Some children simply need a parent to be present, smile occasionally, and tell them they've done a good job.

Parents' attitudes make a difference, too. Do you want to be by your child's side to help, observe, reassure, or direct? Different children, at different ages, respond well to some of these approaches. If your child's needs and yours clash, that will be clear: your child will resist your presence, and your blood pressure will rise. When this happens (and it does happen, at least once, with every child), you need to reevaluate your approach. If practice time is to be shared, it should be pleasant for parents and children.

Motivation versus Bribery

The best way to motivate children to practice is to make clear from the outset that practicing is essential to learning and that you value your child's efforts. Practicing every day is the norm, like brushing teeth and bathing. Expect your child to practice, and make it easy for him or her to find the time. Thank or praise your child for doing a good job. When the habit is in place, it will take little effort to keep it going.

You can use rewards to encourage practicing, but they should not be overdone. The most effective way to use rewards is sparingly, and only for work that exceeds expectations. Rewarding children for doing merely what is expected of them sets the bar too low. The parent who says, "If you practice for thirty minutes every day, I will give you a toy," for example, ensures (at best) that the child will do something with the instrument for half an hour a day, paying more attention to the clock than to the music. It is also unlikely that the child will ever practice without the promise of a toy. And, perhaps most important, the child may never realize that playing an instrument is intrinsically rewarding: that learning a piece, being inspired or captivated by the music, or creating beautiful sounds is really fun.

That is quite different from rewarding accomplishment or unusual effort. One day your child, who has been practicing with reasonable diligence, may independently practice an extra half-hour to complete the memorization of a piece or work out difficult fingering. Or perhaps, midway through a practice session, you hear a "YES!!!" signaling that a persistent problem has been solved. That is the time to say, "Good job! How about an ice-cream cone?" In this case you are encouraging hard work, initiative, and achievement—not just serving time.

Rewards should be small (stickers for young children, special pencils or other school supplies for slightly older kids) and preferably related to music. Teenagers should not need material encouragement. To foster a love of music, you must help your child enjoy listening and playing so that music becomes its own reward. If you can create this attitude toward practicing an instrument, it may carry over into schoolwork and other activities as well.

Deciding When and Where

Parents must provide a certain amount of guidance, even if they plan to participate minimally in daily practice. Where should your child practice? Pianists have no choice, but a portable instrument can be practiced in the living room, the child's bedroom, the kitchen, or even the garage or basement. Some children may want to practice as roving troubadours, wending their way melodically through the house. Help your child choose a way that suits everyone. It is much easier to be supportive of your child's efforts if they blend in with the family's routine. If your child is practicing in solitude, the bedroom will probably work best. With the door shut, the musician need not worry about interruptions or teasing from siblings. If a parent is to be present, which is usually best for younger students, the living room or kitchen will work better. This avoids invading your child's space and ensures a comfortable place for you to sit. It also makes the time for practicing important.

Young children may want the whole family gathered around to admire their musicianship, and for a few days parents and older children may find this cute. The charm will fade rapidly for both sides, though. Besides, even beginners need to learn the difference between practicing and performing. (A monthly home "recital," with cookies and lemonade if you like, should satisfy the need for adulation.) Children may practice in their bedrooms at any time when the rest of the household is awake, but use of the living room should be scheduled at a time that is compatible with the rest of the family's activities. In large families, or small apartments, children may have to learn to concentrate with people walking through the room, doing their homework, or reading. They should not be expected to focus when people in the same room are conversing, watching television, or talking on the phone. It is the parent's job to establish a practice schedule that works for the whole family. If there are several musicians in the house, this may take some negotiation and ingenuity. Younger children may need two shorter practice periods rather than one long session to maintain their concentration.

It is best to choose a regular time and stick to it. Practice is more likely to become a habit, and parents and children are less likely to forget, if a single time is fixed for every day. For example, if 3:30 to 4:00 is always practice time, then it's easy to resolve the question of whether there is time to play a video game or chat with friends. A floating practice time is too easily postponed until no one has the energy to devote to it. A regular practice time commits both child and parent: your child cannot petition for a change without very good reason, but neither can you. Younger children must be entertained elsewhere during practice time so that they do not disturb the practice. If you are working with your practicing child, it is best for younger children to be in another room. Practice time should be just for you and the young musician, if humanly possible. (With any luck, awareness of this special time will provide incentive for younger children to study an instrument, too.) Even if you are not in the practice room, you will need to be at home— at least until your child is old enough to be left alone or in the charge of older siblings.

If a child divides the week between two households, the best time and place to practice may vary from house to house, but it should be consistent in each place. Each parent should attend some lessons, and the child should carry the week's assignment and special instructions (written down) along with the music. It may be easiest for everyone if you simply buy two sets of music.

Being There

Some teachers, especially those who use the Suzuki method, strongly encourage parents to participate in their child's practicing, while others leave the decision entirely up to the family. If you are going to be present while your child practices, you will have to figure out the role that will work best, depending on your abilities and your relationship with your child. You will have to be present at your child's lesson and pay attention so that you know what the teacher wants your child to work on and how. If you know nothing about music, you will at least have to keep up with your child.

At some point (unless you are studying too), your child will know more than you do. That does not mean that you are useless, though. You can still provide encouragement, offer help with counting, and remind about the teacher's instructions. One productive way of helping is to admit your ignorance and ask your child to show or explain something to you. These "teaching" opportunities generate enormous pride in children and also help them internalize and consolidate the material.

If you know a fair amount about music and play the same instrument as your child, you can in theory be very helpful. However, children may become discouraged by the disparity between their parents' abilities and their own. (It's all right for the teacher to be able to play better, but Mom and Dad are different.) Children may resent your ease at doing what is so hard for them. When this happens, you need to step back. Some children, though, are more philosophical. For example, six-year-old Samantha was learning the simple piece called "Clair de Lune" from the first Suzuki book. One day she noticed a piece of her mother's music on the piano with the same name (this one by Debussy). "Mommy, are you playing the same piece?" she asked. Then, turning a few pages and seeing a baffling, intimidating array of notes, she answered her own question: "Oh, no! This one is in cursive!"

Parents with musical training may oftentimes be too demanding. Young children can be expected to have good posture, use correct fingering, play the right notes, and get the rhythm right without being able to achieve the level of musicality you would expect of an older child. Musical parents need to be realistic in their expectations.

Sometimes children are willing to have one parent participate in practicing but not the other, just as they may prefer to have one parent read at bedtime rather than the other. Practicing should be scheduled to make this possible, and the excluded parent should not be insulted. The preference will probably change at some point anyway. And if parents live apart, they will have to recognize that each one has a different relationship with the child, and this affects the interaction during practicing.

Parents may also find that, although they get along beautifully with their children in most situations, the teacher-student relationship does not work very well. If a child prefers to learn independently, rejects assistance with homework, and would rather fall off a bike ten times than accept help—well, the parents had better stay out of the practice room unless invited in. It is probably all right to mention occasionally that something you heard in passing sounded good. (One mother suggested during practice that an F sharp would be better. Her daughter replied, "I like F natural." Mom said, "Mozart liked F sharp," and the child answered, "On Saturday we'll see what my teacher likes." A conversation like that is certainly a clear signal to stay completely out of the room.)

As children grow older and more accomplished, the parent's role in practicing diminishes. Older children need to gain more independence and take more responsibility for their practicing. No parent should be sitting alongside a teenager supervising either the duration of the practice session or the accuracy of the intonation. Older children are more likely to need their parents' help managing their time, setting priorities, and making decisions about competitions and performances. If they ask your advice or your opinion about their playing, by all means respond (tactfully but honestly). Unsolicited advice should be reserved for genuine problems.

Children sometimes become frustrated when they practice. This is understandable: fingers don't always do what they're told. Usually one of the practicing techniques your child has learned can stop a pattern of repeated error. That is, if a child cannot get a passage right, then playing each hand separately (on the piano), clapping the rhythm or counting aloud, playing one measure at a time, or some other approach can end an impasse. A reminder that there are other ways to work on a problem may be all that is needed. Parents can (and should) intervene before the child's frustration reaches the point of screaming, tantrums, or tears. Although it is best to work out these difficulties, sometimes the only solution is to switch to another piece and not return to the problem until the next day or even the next lesson.

If a child's frustration grows out of unrealistic expectations or perfectionism, chances are that music is not the only area in which this characteristic appears. It is important to recognize that this personality trait propels children toward both achievement and misery. If it can be moderated, children can continue to succeed but become happier and easier to live with. The music teacher can help your child set realistic goals (for example, your child may not be quite ready for the Chopin prelude someone played at the recital) and reasonable standards of performance. One of the wonderful things about music is that you can always get better: there is always room for improvement, even in the simplest piece. A ten-year-old may play one of Bach's little preludes very well—but not yet as well as Canadian pianists Glenn Gould or Angela Hewitt. If a perfection-seeking child can learn that lesson, and rejoice in improvement rather than perfection, music lessons (once again) will have been worth twice their price.

And When They Don't . . .

Every child will skip practicing from time to time. Do you work out every day? Always floss? Never leave the dishes in the sink? Occasional forgetfulness or laziness is nothing to worry about. When children simply refuse to practice for days on end, or when practice time becomes a pitched battle, it's time for action.

First, is practicing really what the rebellion is about? Often, not practicing is just the easiest way to assert independence, control, or contrariness. If your child is going through a transition at school, the physical changes of adolescence (or even just a growth spurt), or a struggle with parents or siblings over some other issue, practicing may become just one more skirmish in a larger war. The best solution is to deal with the root cause (if possible) or just wait it out. If you can't solve the larger problem, you may be able to put practicing on neutral ground by making a deal with your child. "I know you don't feel like practicing, but it's only two months until your recital. If you just work hard on your recital piece, then you'll be able to play well." Then, of course, your child's teacher can point out that the trills in the recital piece can only be improved by practicing an exercise, and that practicing the scales in the key of the recital piece would help with fingering. Rebellion will break out elsewhere (a messy room, whining about chores, neglected homework), but the practicing will get done.

Sometimes, however, a refusal to practice really is about practicing. We will talk about ending music lessons in chapter 9, and there are good reasons to stop. But let's assume for now that those reasons are not present. First, see whether the time set for practicing needs to be changed. If there is a TV show that your child cannot miss without becoming a social outcast, then practice time can be moved. Your child may need a quick nap after school (teenagers need more sleep than they often get). If so, postpone practicing until after naptime. Children may also feel a great deal of pressure to get their school homework done early, especially if they are afraid of (or eager to please) an especially demanding teacher. Postponing practice time until after dinner can give the child time for homework, relieve some of the pressure, and make practice time more relaxed.

Your child may dislike one piece of music. If so, the child should raise this with the teacher, who can decide whether it is essential (scales fall into this category) or optional (another exercise can always be substituted). Usually, however, you will just have to accept the fact that your child is temporarily in nonpracticing mode. Discuss the problem with the teacher and decide whether to ignore it (and for how long) or to work at changing it. The problem may disappear faster if the parent ignores it but the teacher pursues it.

Whether parents should try to enforce practicing depends to a great extent on the child's age. Once children reach the age of eleven or twelve, discussions about practicing should generally be left to the child and the teacher, with parents involved only at the request of one of them. The ability to practice independently, and to face the consequences of not practicing, is part of maturing and becoming responsible. If a child seeks help, though, be sure to provide it. It is a sign of maturity when your child says, "I want to practice, but I know I'll let it go if you don't remind me. Please tell me to practice if I forget." Agree to do the reminding—on the condition that your child will accept the reminder graciously.

Beyond Practicing

Children's musical experience does not begin at the first music lesson. From the day we are born, we hear music around us. We remember a mother's lullaby, nursery songs from kindergarten, popular songs from our teenage years, and favorite Broadway show tunes or movie soundtracks. We are immersed in music, whether it is classical, jazz, country, pop, or elevator. With so many choices, styles, and genres, it is easy to get lost. What should we offer to our children? We typically introduce them first to what we like and listen to ourselves, but we should also offer them other options, even if we are not familiar or comfortable with them. Parents and children can learn together. They may even discover something new that will bring them closer together.

It is worth making some effort to understand your child's musical tastes, but some musical choices will cause conflict. Teenagers often prefer to listen to music that makes their parents cringe. Indeed, that may be the purpose of their choices. Teenagers assert their independence through their tastes in clothing, hairstyles, and vocabulary. Music is one more way to show that they are not Mom and Dad. Nevertheless, it is important to talk about music with your children. Ask their opinions about the music they like, find out what appeals to them and why, and what feelings or thoughts the music evokes. Tell them what you like and why. Listen to music together and discuss it. Dealing with musical rebellion is no harder (or easier) than dealing with other varieties. Let children listen to their own choices, but don't let them impose those choices on you or your neighbors. Rules about when music may be played, and at what volume, are easiest to enforce. This focus makes the issue one of being considerate of others, rather than one of parents imposing their outdated musical tastes. Headphones are also useful.

Listening to well-performed music will improve your child's ear and remind everyone what all the hard work of practicing can lead to. And there are other ways to participate in music that can also be useful and fun. Most small children have a tape player of some kind. Indeed, many music teachers tape pieces for their students to listen to. Tapes are inexpensive and can often be borrowed from the library. These tapes may be especially for children or just recordings of music that your child will enjoy. If you have a CD player, there is a nearly endless supply of good music available.

There is also good music on radio and television. PBS broadcasts a wide variety of concerts, as do some cable stations. These are sometimes shown after most children's bedtimes, but you can tape these programs if you have a VCR. The first time your child hears a piece from his or her own repertoire on the radio is unforgettable: you can almost hear her thinking, "I'm playing real music! I'm a real musician!"

If you live in the suburbs, you probably spend a lot of time in the car with your child. The classical radio station, tapes, or a CD can make every traffic jam a concert. Well, almost. In any case, classical music is less likely to contribute to road rage than most other genres. If you or your child prefers rock or jazz, listen to that. If you can't agree, take turns. The important thing is to listen.

Live music is the best. Whether the pleasure comes from actually seeing real musicians up close, or the atmosphere of the concert hall, or being with other listeners, or just getting dressed up and going somewhere special with parents, concerts are very special occasions for children. They need not be expensive. There are usually some free or inexpensive performances, and most concerts offer student ticket rates. If you live near a college or university, you can get their concert schedule; most of these performances are free. Orchestras often have special programs for children (often free), where they can meet members of the orchestra, learn about an instrument, or listen to a rehearsal (a great way to reinforce the value of practicing). Youth orchestras are especially inspiring for young musicians. These programs are easy to investigate. Sometimes musical groups make free tickets available to young people through schools, music teachers, or Boys & Girls Clubs. Take advantage of as many of these options as your schedule allows.

By listening to recorded music, your child may develop a special liking for a certain performer. If so, a ticket to a performance if that person is coming to your town makes a much-valued gift. If no performance is available, a recording or a poster (usually available from the artist's recording company, and sometimes autographed) is a good substitute.

Singing—whether alone, in a family group, or with friends—also develops your child's ear and sense of rhythm, as well as pleasure in music. If your own voice is not ready for a Carnegie Hall recital, you can still sing with your child in the car, in the kitchen, or wherever you are comfortable. Dancing, too, develops rhythm and offers your child another way to enjoy music. If your child is especially energetic, dancing is one of the least objectionable ways of burning off some of the excess.

With daily practice sessions, recorded music, the car radio, and frequent concert attendance, music quickly becomes a large part of your family's life. Many parents seek out music lessons for their children because they grew up with music. For others, this is an entirely new and exciting experience. Your child's music lessons can bring the pleasure of encountering and living with music to the whole family.

chapter 7:

COMPETITIONS, RECITALS, AND OTHER PERFORMANCES

The competition movement in music may be described in a general way as an effort to harness man's love of sport to the interest of his cultivation of art.

—The Oxford Companion to Music

An important part of music education is learning to share the enjoyment of music and accomplishment with others. This sharing takes many forms: playing for friends and family, performing in class recitals, playing in ensembles, and participating in city, regional, and national recitals and competitions. All of these opportunities benefit students in different ways, and understanding how they work will help parents guide children into appropriate opportunities.

The history of music competitions can be traced as far back as Greek mythology, when Pan vied with Phoebus to see who was the better flutist. Many books and articles have been dedicated to the subject, but in this chapter we focus on competitions for precollege students. If not carefully considered, competitions can take the fun out of music and replace pleasure with anxiety. If students wish to compete, they should be properly prepared. And if they do not wish to enter competitions, parents and teachers can help them find other opportunities to perform.

Most local music competitions are sponsored by the state music teachers' organizations. To enter a student in a competition, a teacher must be a member in good standing. Some local competitions are held in the format of a festival with a theme: a sonatina, ragtime, or jazz festival; a concerto competition; or a competition featuring the music of a specific period or composer. Some competitions and festivals include recitals that don't offer prizes but do provide a written evaluation of the participant's performance. Often, as part of the program, they offer master classes and solo recitals given by guest artists who may also serve as judges. Some competitions have two or three rounds, and some select finalists from audiotapes or videotapes. Some are open to the public, while others are closed, except for the semifinal or final rounds.

Most competitions divide students according to age or grade in school. Teachers are generally provided with lists or types of compositions that are appropriate for each age group. Typical divisions are beginning elementary, advanced elementary, junior high school, and senior high school. Students may need to prepare two or more pieces from different musical periods or styles. There are almost always limits on the length of the performance.

Winners are selected by a group of judges, and awards range from written evaluations, certificates, and trophies to cash prizes, medals, and performance opportunities. Some competitions do not have the traditional first, second, and third places. Instead, a group of winners is chosen and rated "superior with distinction," "superior," or "honorable mention," with a few students placing in each category. Still other competitions reward a group of unranked winners. Sometimes gold, silver, and bronze medals are awarded. Such competitions are much kinder than those with only one or two winners. The goal for precollege competitions is to educate and to reward hard work, dedication, and talent.

Competitions are almost always surrounded by controversy. Judges' decisions, based on their own tastes, preferences, and experiences, are highly subjective, and audiences more often than not disagree with the judges (and not simply in favor of their own children or their teacher's other students). Violinist Arnold Steinhardt, who won the prestigious Leventritt Competition in 1958, has described the problem: "The only avenue that seemed open to me was a prestigious violin competition: win one of these and you were given concerts, even money, and a certain amount of publicity. But it was an awful business. You were a nag in a horse race with a number on your back. There's nothing wrong with a real horse race—the first one across the finish line wins—but how does one judge a musical entrant in a competition? By how fast he plays? How few mistakes he makes? How does one grade beauty, after all?"

However, competitions do have certain merits and, if approached correctly, may benefit students. Pianist Alfred Brendel, who came from a nonmusical family, explains the psychological benefits of winning a major prize, in this case at the 1949 Busoni Competition, when he was eighteen: "It was becoming more and more apparent that I should be a pianist, but the prize was a confirmation. And the recognition was particularly meaningful to my parents, who did not know the musical scene at all, and who were naturally very skeptical about a career which offered no security."

Advantages and Disadvantages

The advantages of participating in competitions include learning and polishing fresh repertoire (including new composers), receiving judges' evaluations and constructive criticism that may be valuable for future musical development, enhancing self-discipline and focus, meeting and hearing other performers, gaining a feeling of accomplishment, acquiring opportunities to perform, winning a scholarship, and setting new short- and long-term goals. Today's competitors may be tomorrow's colleagues in a regional ensemble. And the excitement of victory may become an inspiration for future achievement.

Yet competing has at least as many disadvantages. One of the most important issues to consider before entering students in a competition is whether they are emotionally ready to handle criticism or "losing" and whether they are physically and musically ready for the challenge. This is especially important for young children who are competing for the first time. Negative comments from the judges, teacher, or parents may damage a child's sense of self-worth and be traumatic for many years. The child's teacher should analyze the judges' critique and discuss it with the student. Negative comments should be turned into positive suggestions for learning from one's mistakes.

"Losing" a competition, if handled correctly, may have a very positive outcome. We do not win everything we want in life, but by learning how to overcome our loss, embarrassment, and wounded ego, we become stronger and appreciate our achievements. In the long run, this is more important than winning a gold medal in a local competition.

"Winning," if handled incorrectly, may have a negative outcome. Some winners get such a high from the victory that they want to participate in every competition there is, and they begin to measure their achievements by the number of medals they have won, neglecting their studies and losing sight of their own goals. For these students, losing a competition (which they inevitably will) may be devastating, humiliating, and damaging beyond repair.

Another disadvantage of competitions is that focusing exclusively on preparing for a competition may limit a student's repertoire and participation in other musical and nonmusical activities. Extended hours of practice for competitions may deprive a child of much-needed sleep and lead to emotional and physical exhaustion.

Who, then, should decide whether a child should participate in a competition: the student, the parent, or the teacher? Of course, no student should be coerced into entering a competition. The decision must begin with the student's willingness (preferably eagerness) to compete. Often parents are more eager to enter their children in music competitions than are the children themselves. Some become so involved in the competition business and in collecting trophies that it becomes an obsession. Parents who do not have any musical background may not fully understand how damaging this approach can be. If you are a parent of a talented, hard-working student and want your child to participate in a competition, have a talk with your child's teacher about the child's readiness for such a challenge. It is the teacher's role to decide whether a student is a good candidate, especially if the child is young and entering a competition for the first time. The first experience is very important and should be as positive as possible. The teacher knows not only your child's ability but also the general ability level of other children likely to enter a given competition, as well as the way the competition is conducted and judged.

Some children who enjoy music lessons and performing for relatives and friends may not do well under the pressure and public exposure of competitions. Others love the challenge and are inspired by it. It is the teacher's responsibility to assess a student's emotional, physical, and professional readiness, as well as his or her motivation. It is also the teacher's responsibility to choose appropriate repertoire that is within the competition's guidelines and the student's reach.

A decision to participate in a competition cannot and should not be spontaneous. It must be thoroughly examined well in advance. The best results can be achieved if the student's repertoire is collected over a period of time, tested in recitals and other performances, and then finely polished for a particular competition. Freshly learned pieces that a student has just put together and that have not yet settled can lead to devastating, embarrassing performances with memory lapses and technical problems, often resulting in stage fright and other emotional problems. Students will feel more confident, and will enjoy competitions more, if they are well prepared and have their teacher's strong endorsement. If they know they have worked hard and done their best, winning or losing is not the most important thing.

Recitals

The goal of music lessons is not winning a competition but opening a door to the fascinating world of music, learning to decipher and understand the mysterious language of music, becoming an educated listener, playing an instrument, accompanying a chorus, singing, or just enjoying others' performances. A good alternative to performing in competitions is performing in recitals. (Recitals can also serve as rehearsals for competitions.) Often, recitals—like competitions—are dedicated to a certain theme, such as the music of a particular composer, period, or form. Recitals are open to performers of all ages, levels, and skills. Like competitions, recitals require polished performance, but participants are not rated or ranked. Many students prefer playing in this challenging but noncompetitive setting.

Most teachers hold annual or semiannual class recitals in which all students may participate, if they are adequately prepared. If a studio is large, teachers may divide students into smaller performance groups, usually by level: beginning, intermediate, and advanced. Beginning students are strongly urged to attend the more advanced performances. These are sometimes their only opportunity to hear accomplished performers, and such performances can be very exciting and inspiring for the little ones. They are exposed to new music played by their peers, and they often ask the teacher when they will be able to play this or that piece.

It may happen that during a competition or recital, a student will experience the magic of completely merging with the music, a kind of hypnosis that ends with the last note. It is a moment so powerful and incredible that one may feel transported to a different world. Musicians who experience such moments of inspiration will continue searching for them again and again. This magic spreads to members of the audience, who observe in awe the birth of a real artist. Both artist and audience will dissolve in music. This does not happen very often, especially at junior-level performances, but when it does, it is an unforgettable moment in the lives of everyone present, especially the performer. Cellist and novelist Mark Salzman offers a fictional music teacher's account of such a moment:

> While Kyung-hee played, the music seemed to have hands that reached into my chest, took a firm grip and shook me savagely—so hard that I felt as though I were really waking up from a dream. . . . When I opened my eyes and looked around me, what I saw was a tiny boy playing the cello, and I felt engulfed, swept away by something immediately familiar.

It was the experience of music I had felt almost every day for the first half of my life. As he played I remembered what it felt like to be playing the music myself. . . . It's so simple and so obvious: when he plays, the music goes into my ears, resonates in my mind and becomes a part of me! It becomes my music too.

Such experiences can be dreamed of and hoped for, but they cannot be summoned up at will. And they can only happen when the performer knows the music so well that music and performer become one.

Parents can organize their own home recitals, inviting family and friends as an audience, with a few children (your own and perhaps those of the neighbors) to perform, possibly on different instruments. You can reward the performers with small prizes, such as sweets and small toys. Arnold Steinhardt has remembered these occasions fondly: "Our own house often served as an unlikely concert hall. . . . I would show off my latest wares, a salon piece to touch the heart, or a virtuoso work that dazzled and impressed. Oohs, ahs, and smothering hugs were the rewards." If you ask your child to play for your friends, be careful not to get into show-off mode. Some children may resent being put on display, and then you will never get them to perform. If you are casual about it, they will respond better. Other children, though, like to show off what they have learned. Let them enjoy it, but know when to stop. Otherwise you may find yourself short of friends willing to visit your home.

Schools and Community Centers

Schools often have talent shows where students can perform for one another and for teachers. These provide an opportunity for children to share their accomplishments with their peers. If possible, encourage younger children to think of these performances as sharing their pleasure in music rather than showing off. The other students will be just as impressed, and the young musician will be less likely to be teased.

One of the most gratifying places for young children to perform is a senior center or nursing home. Older people love little kids and are the most forgiving and admiring audience in the world. You can bring the most insecure performers to a nursing home and have the joy of seeing them leave feeling like superstars. As an added benefit, the children will know that they have brought joy to someone's life. Always encourage your child to perform in any nonjudgmental, informal setting, but don't force it. If a child is not secure about playing, sets high standards for performance, and is forced to perform, the result may be just as devastating as losing a competition.

Nerves

The more a young student plays in front of an audience, the more comfortable he or she will be on stage, and the less likelihood there is of stage fright and nervousness. Very young students are usually completely comfortable playing before the public. As they grow older, however, they often become more self-conscious and nervous during performances. This can become a serious problem, and it needs to be addressed from the beginning. Saying "Don't be nervous" does not help. Asking "Are you nervous?" is even worse. Do not even consider giving medication to solve the problem.

When students say they are nervous before a performance, tell them that it is okay to be nervous on such occasions, that in fact it is normal. All artists are nervous before performances. The trick is to turn nervousness into excitement. As pianist Madeline Bruser has pointed out, "Fear is energy. If you allow it to flow through you, you transform it into fearlessness." If you are not nervous or excited, then you are indifferent to the music you are playing and your performance will be flat and boring. Focus only on the music, not on the audience or the judges, and not on yourself.

There are different reasons for nervousness. The most common are technical insecurities, fear of forgetting the notes, and fear of embarrassing oneself, one's parents, or one's teacher in front of peers, an audience, or judges. On this point, Josef Hofmann has said, "Are you quite sure that your 'nervousness' is not merely another name for self-consciousness, or worse yet, for a 'bad conscience' on the score of technical security? In the latter case you ought to perfect your technique, while in the former you must learn to discard all thought of your dear self, as well as of your hearers in relation to you, and concentrate your thinking upon the work you are to do."

Great performers share this philosophy and admit to having pre-concert jitters. Some have developed their own exercises and techniques to help overcome nervousness. The best treatments for the jitters are:

- Be well prepared (pianist and conductor Vladimir Ashkenazy says that "working hard at practice is also the best defense I know against preconcert nervousness").
- Focus on the music you are performing.
- Get excited about sharing your talent and music with others.

Other practical methods for dealing with nerves include playing the program in informal settings before family or friends as often as possible. Students should be well rested on the day of the performance and should eat a light but nutritious meal beforehand. It is a good idea for children to express their fears to their parents or teacher. Sometimes just by saying them out loud, they will resolve any doubts or worries.

Very young performers' stage fright or butterflies may be caused by fear of disappointing their parents or displeasing their teacher. Parents who are trying to encourage their children to do their best may inadvertently put too much pressure on them. For example, when five-year-old Danny, a gifted little boy, was preparing for his first public recital, he played his piece for the teacher at his lesson and said, "My father said I must play brilliantly. Was it brilliant?" "No, not yet," replied the teacher. After a thoughtful pause, Danny asked, "Was it half brilliant?" Reassure children of your love and tell them that you are proud of them just for having the courage to perform in front of all these people or judges. Be supportive and understanding. Do not show your disappointment in their nervousness or in any bad effect it has on their performance.

Some parents are more nervous than their children. They cannot eat before a competition or recital, and they sit through what should be an enjoyable occasion with tense muscles and white knuckles. Parents' anxiety can be contagious. Children may perceive it as a lack of confidence in them (or they may simply dismiss it as Dad's weirdness). Parents need to adopt the attitude they are urging on their children: this is a time to enjoy your child's accomplishments and those of other children. Winning is less important than doing one's best, and making mistakes will not cause the sky to fall. If parents cannot conquer their nervousness, they should do their best to hide it. The mother of one extremely talented young musician became so nervous about competitions (even though her daughter almost invariably won) that the whole family agreed she would not attend. She avoided making her daughter nervous, but she also missed some wonderful performances.

Parents and Performance

Parents have certain practical responsibilities when their children perform in recitals or competitions. They must study the guidelines of the event carefully and clarify all confusing questions well in advance by asking the child's teacher or an official of the event. They must fill out the application form and file it on time, along with any application fees. Parents must hire an accompanist for the child if necessary—again, well in advance. Parents should be careful not to schedule any other activities earlier on the day of the performance, and they should not allow the child to attend any late-night events or slumber parties the night before. Young performers need to get enough sleep.

On the day of the event, parents should help children to dress appropriately. Some competitions have dress codes that include rules about skirt lengths and other details. Parents should plan this in advance and not worry children unnecessarily by leaving ironing or hemming to the last minute. Parents should make sure they know how to get to the recital hall and leave plenty of time for travel, double-checking in advance the time that their child is expected. Children should have time to warm up before the performance. In general, parents should be well prepared and organized so that unnecessary conflicts, worries, and delays do not contribute to the child's anxiety. They should be positive, encouraging, and supportive.

The parents' job does not end with the performance. Parents play an important role after the recital or competition is over. If the event went well, share in your child's joy. Call family members, celebrate (perhaps with dinner at your child's favorite restaurant), and make your child feel special. Let your child know how proud you are, but be realistic about the importance of the event. Do not exaggerate the significance of a competition, and help your child draw the line between justifiable pride and arrogance.

It is more difficult, of course, to deal with "failure" or the perception of failure. Success and failure are relative terms. For one child the mere fact of overcoming stage fright and having the courage to play in front of the audience may be a huge success and personal victory. Another child may consider getting a silver medal instead of a gold one a terrible failure. If your child's performance really did not go well, do not lie. It is a mistake to say, "It was wonderful, Honey. I'm so proud of you." Children know the truth and will never believe false praise. Instead, parents and teachers should work "in concert," explaining to the young student that being chosen as a participant is an honor and that it is important to learn from our mistakes, work hard, improve, and try again. Talk to your child and together try to understand the reason for the poor performance. Talk to the teacher and try to pinpoint the problem. Was it stage fright, poor preparation, lack of concentration, inappropriate repertoire, or some other problem?

What do you say to a child who played his or her best in a competition but did not place? Prepare your child for this possibility before the competition. Explain that it is important to focus on doing your best, and that winning is not as important as how you feel about your performance afterward. Selection of winners is, after all, a subjective opinion of two or three judges. Another set of judges might have a different opinion. After the competition, carefully read the judges' comments and discuss them with the teacher. Do not criticize or diminish the judges. Together with your child, attend the winners' recital to understand the judges' criteria better. And remember a simple truth: another child may be more talented than your child, or better prepared, or a more interesting performer. Think of the big international competitions. Nobody makes obvious "mistakes"; everybody is well prepared, technically equipped, and very professional; yet at the end of the third round only a handful of performers are left and even fewer win an award. Can anyone really measure the difference between a gold and a silver performance?

Many great musicians never participated in competitions or received any medals, but they nevertheless have brilliant careers. "If the pianists are any good, they don't need a competition," said Spanish pianist Alicia de Larrocha. The most talented performers often do not win competitions, and some winners do not develop into interesting artists and are forgotten within a few years. We will give world-renowned pianist Vladimir Horowitz the last word: "Another element that is capable of hurting the artist is the competitions. From a managerial standpoint, it helps to capitalize, to have a winner, and then launch a career. But from the musical point of view, I don't like them because they select not by excellence, but by elimination. There was a big competition at the end of the nineteenth century. I believe it was the Anton Rubinstein Competition in Moscow. Busoni played and took third prize. First prize was won by Mr. Heinz. Do you know who Busoni is? Do you know who Heinz is?"

chapter 8:

BAND, ORCHESTRA, AND CHOIR

When a performance is in progress,
all four of us together enter a zone of magic
somewhere between our music stands and become
conduit, messenger, and missionary.
—**Arnold Steinhardt,** *Indivisible by Four*

P laying music with others, whether in school or at home, enhances a student's experience both musically and socially. Performing in an ensemble demands precision in rhythm and intonation and increases appreciation of dynamics. It allows musicians who can play only one note at a time to hear harmony and polyphony. Playing in ensembles also teaches cooperation and teamwork: it gives instrumentalists and singers an opportunity to work together, usually with a director, to create music that no single performer can create alone.

For most young people, belonging to a school band, orchestra, or choir is the best way to perform in ensembles. These musical activities usually begin in middle school or junior high, although elementary schools may have vocal or percussion ensembles. Students' experiences will depend on how well they play their instruments at the outset, on their general musical training, and on the quality of their peers and teachers.

A child who has already begun a band or orchestra instrument will probably be able to play an important role in middle school musical groups. A relatively accomplished violinist may take the first chair in the orchestra and be in a position to lead and coach less experienced players. The young wind performer with a few years of lessons may become a celebrity in band class. In a school where many students play instruments, though, there may be serious competition for those positions; by high school, this is a certainty. Children need to be prepared, both musically and psychologically, to audition and to live with the results. There is, after all, only one first chair, and as composer Robert Schumann pointed out, "If all were determined to play the first violin, we should never have complete orchestras."

Although band and orchestra teachers may dream of classes filled with able performers, they do not want prima donnas. Ensemble playing is a team effort, and children will enjoy it more—and perform better—if they understand this. Parents will naturally encourage children and help them do well in auditions, but it is equally important to help them understand that every member of the group is vital. Competitiveness is vital for competitions and auditions but counterproductive in day-to-day rehearsals and in performances.

It is especially important for the most able and the least able performers to understand the importance of cooperation. An accomplished young musician may not be at all challenged—indeed, may be a bit bored—in a school band or orchestra when the music played is far less challenging than the pieces she or he practices for lessons. For this child, the group experience is an opportunity to lead, set an example, help others, develop an ensemble repertoire, and work on whatever special skills or techniques the orchestral music requires. Even the best solo performer has a great deal to learn about ensemble playing.

Students who are barely able to keep up with the group may have other problems: frustration, embarrassment, and a need to work far harder than others. Parents can help these students by encouraging them and, if they know how, working with them to improve skills. From time to time, the private music teacher may modify the teaching plan to help the student with an ensemble problem. Certainly the teacher will take time to answer the student's questions about specific pieces. Some students playing in school ensembles do not take private lessons. The instruction provided by the band or orchestra teacher is the only help they receive. Any child receiving private instruction who practices with reasonable diligence should catch up with the group quickly.

Sometimes a student decides to use band or orchestra to experiment with a second instrument. You can't play the cello or piano in a marching band. Chapter 4 discusses the special considerations about beginning a second instrument. But there is one important thing to remember about experienced student musicians who join a school group with a brand new instrument: they already have some basic musical competence that will help them. They know how to count and read music, and they know the musical terms used to direct performers about tempo and dynamics. A firm grounding in music theory will help no matter what the instrument.

A strong musical background also helps students who join the choir. Reading notes for singing is, of course, quite different than reading notes for playing an instrument. After all, there is no key or string to press or hole to cover to produce the right note. However, students can practice singing along with the piano or a string instrument. Some instrumental teachers also teach sightsinging to help students develop a better ear for pitch.

Music in School

Musical instruction should begin in preschool and kindergarten. The youngest children can be taught rhythm by playing drums, triangles, and other percussion instruments, and they can sing, dance, or perform other rhythmic movements. Some schools have adopted sophisticated music programs; those based on the theories of composers Carl Orff and Zoltán Kodály are the best known. Older children continue with their singing and learn to read music. Some schools also teach music appreciation and music history. Other schools even give students an opportunity to experiment with a variety of musical instruments.

Basic music classes in which students do not perform can teach a great deal. First, students can learn to listen to music. They can learn to distinguish among instruments, to pick out the melodic line, to identify a variety of rhythms, and to recognize different styles, composers, and compositions. Second, they can learn basic theory: reading notes; building scales, intervals, and chords; and clapping rhythms. Third, they can learn musical terms, forms, and history. Fourth, they can develop their own tastes in music. Finally, students can learn to verbalize their knowledge so that they can talk intelligently about music and express their tastes and opinions. If your school has a comprehensive music program that teaches all of these things, your child is extremely fortunate—and the rare exception in the United States. Most elementary and middle schools teach little about music, however, and most high schools offer only music performance classes that may—if the teacher has time—include some theory and history.

Unfortunately, many school systems regard music as a luxury and have dropped formal music instruction from the curriculum entirely. If you can prevent this from happening in your school system, or can reverse the decision, we urge you to do so. Some of the groups listed in "For Further Information" provide suggestions for encouraging school administrators to provide music instruction. If your child's elementary school does not provide formal musical instruction and does not have a music teacher, there are still many ways to bring music into the classroom. Ask your child's teacher about playing recorded music during quiet times in school, such as silent reading. Parents can volunteer to lend CDs or tapes (almost every school has a tape recorder), and even teachers who know nothing about music can adapt the liner notes to the children's level of understanding. Some orchestras, chamber groups, and choral groups have programs that send musicians into schools to talk about and demonstrate their instruments, or to perform and talk to students. Parents can investigate these possibilities and let teachers know how to make these opportunities available to the children. Young children who take music lessons may wish to perform for their classmates, and show-and-tell time can be made available to them. Talent shows can boost children's pride and confidence, and they provide an opportunity to acknowledge accomplishments that might otherwise go unrecognized. Music is too important to be excluded from a child's early education.

In middle schools, junior high schools, and small high schools, a single teacher usually teaches band, orchestra, and choir. In large high schools, each subject may be taught by a different teacher. Very large schools will have ensembles organized according to the students' abilities, ranging from beginning to honors. Some schools even have special coaches for different sections and instruments.

Band, orchestra, and choir classes are not music lessons. Even the best-trained, most accomplished teacher will be truly proficient on only one or two instruments. The band teacher who plays the clarinet can offer advice to the flutist or trombonist but cannot be expected to teach the instrument. Choral teachers should be accomplished vocal coaches, but they, too, are dealing with many students at various levels of talent and experience. Few students take voice lessons, so there are rarely any well-trained singers to set an example. Nor is there time for the teacher to work individually with students. The teacher is working with the ensemble, sometimes section by section, to get the notes right, to set a uniform tempo, to balance the dynamics, and to make it all sound like music. As members of the group, students learn to do all of these things and how to contribute to the music with their own instruments or voices. They must learn to watch the conductor, understand and follow direction, and listen to the other ensemble members—both in their own section and in the others. Ensemble playing is very different from solo performance, and it is hard work.

Parents sometimes do not know what to expect from school music classes. In school, children should be learning ensemble skills and a commitment to ensemble playing. When children talk about band or orchestra, they should be speaking in the first-person plural: "*We* played really well today" or "Mr. Sanders made *our* section play the first ten measures about a million times." As long as your child is clearly working well as part of the group and is enjoying the experience most of the time, and if the group's performance is improving, the teacher is doing a good job. If your child is seriously committed to a musical career, you will need to find a setting that provides more of a challenge, whether a regional group or a small ensemble.

One danger to watch out for is the ensemble that is driven entirely by a performance schedule. Performance is important for many reasons—including motivation, experience, and public relations—but if students are performing too frequently, basic instructional goals may not be met. The number of extra rehearsals may also become excessive. This usually becomes a problem for the highest-level groups, whose members are already more likely to be involved in extracurricular music. If band or orchestra is not your child's primary extracurricular commitment, an ensemble that performs less frequently may work better.

Band, orchestra, and choir are in some ways like other classes, and problems may arise. If they do, try to determine the source of the problem. Parents can step in just as they would in any other class: get the facts and meet with the teacher. If this does not resolve the problem, parents may need to meet with the principal or other administrator.

One Student, Two Teachers

Taking music lessons and playing in a school ensemble should complement each other in developing a child's musical skills. Your child will still need to practice for lessons. Practice for band or orchestra is the equivalent of homework in math or English and does not substitute for regular practicing. The extent to which your child's music teacher becomes involved in the ensemble work can range from not at all to quite a bit, and this may vary depending on the priorities of the moment. The parent, the child, and the teacher can discuss this and reach an understanding.

Conflict between a music teacher and the band or orchestra teacher is unlikely: they are not teaching the same things and have very different relationships with their students. However, you may find them competing for your child's time, at least indirectly. For example, the band teacher may tell your child to practice more and improve his performance or risk being demoted to a less demanding group or receiving a lower grade. If your child's response is to sacrifice practicing for lessons in favor of practicing for band, the results will become apparent fairly quickly. Middle school children will feel caught between two powerful adults, and they do not have the skills to handle such situations. Parents need to step in and help negotiate. High school students may feel able to resolve these difficulties, but parents should at least be kept informed about what is happening and should step in when appropriate, even over the child's protests.

Seventy-Six Trombones

Encouraging your child to play in the high school band or sing in the choir is frequently promoted as a way of keeping kids out of trouble. Indeed, there are fewer more angelic-looking children than flutists and choirboys. Unfortunately we cannot claim that playing music automatically leads to good behavior. Students on band trips need to be chaperoned as carefully as those traveling to debate tournaments and basketball games. We can claim some social and behavioral benefits from school music, though—benefits that other group activities share.

Students who participate in musical groups are part of a team and derive all the benefits team sports offer. They learn good sportsmanship (how to win or lose a competition, or a chair, gracefully), getting along with others, and the risks and benefits of interdependence. Band morale is no less real than football team morale, though it tends to be more tastefully expressed. Musicians usually make good friends among fellow band, orchestra, or choir members. They go out for pizza after rehearsals, call each other on the phone or send instant messages on the Internet, and participate in arranged group activities. Most high school students join a group for social support; band, choir, and orchestra offer these opportunities in abundance. The quality of musicianship—whether the individual's or the group's—has little relevance to the quality of the group experience. The band that wins all the competitions will enjoy the attention and status, just as the championship football team does. Not every school music group, though, can win all the prizes. For most, their group spirit comes from working and playing together, mastering new music, and sharing experiences, jokes, and good times.

There are two reasons that school musicians tend to stay out of trouble. The first is that they are busy and don't have time to hang out at the pool hall, video arcade, or other den of adolescent vice. The second is that their parents are usually very much involved in their activities. If your daughter is in the band, you will probably know all the kids she hangs out with—and their parents.

Time

Band, choir, and orchestra occupy a student's time outside school. There are often rehearsals before or after school, as well as performances on and off campus. The orchestra may rehearse late into the night when playing for the drama club's musical comedy. Marching band takes many hours of practice, usually early in the morning, and requires performance at football games, pep rallies, and other occasions. Students may also become involved in other ensembles—small jazz, rock, or classical groups or a cappella choirs that they arrange on their own outside school, or city, regional, or state bands and orchestras. These, too, require time for individual practice, group rehearsal, and performance. Participants will need their parents' help with transportation, organization, and business transactions. Band, orchestra, and choir groups offer a source of friendships and of positive group loyalty. "Band kids" often sit together at lunch and socialize after school and on weekends. These are healthy relationships that parents should encourage, but there are only twenty-four hours in a day.

Your child's decision to continue music lessons through high school and to play seriously in school and extracurricular ensembles is a major commitment of time and effort. It probably precludes involvement in any other time-consuming activity, like an intramural sport or the debate team. High school students need to be developing the ability to make such decisions for themselves, but it is the parent's responsibility to bring a little realism into the process. It may also be necessary to work with your child to develop better time-management skills.

All of a child's musical activities consume parents' time, just as sports and other school activities do. Even if you can reduce chauffeur duty by carpooling with other parents, you will want to attend your child's performances. Flutist Paula Robison remembers that her parents "always came to whatever I did, even in junior high school when I played second flute in the orchestra and I had two little notes to play—they were listening to the notes!" Children value their parents' presence as an expression of interest, pride, and love.

You are likely to receive requests for you and your child to participate in fundraising activities to finance uniforms and special trips, especially for marching bands. These activities take time, and many parents find them unpleasant. Your child's musical group may be invited to perform out of state or even abroad, and you will have to trust your child, the other students, and the chaperones to meet the standards of behavior and safety that you are comfortable with. Or you may have to volunteer as a chaperone yourself! You should not encourage your child to join school musical groups if you cannot provide the necessary logistical and moral support. If playing in an ensemble is important to your child, be prepared to make the necessary effort and sacrifices.

Ensembles Outside School

Although most young musicians do their ensemble playing in school, they can also take advantage of other opportunities ranging from statewide orchestras to small, independent groups. Students may also wish to participate in summer programs that include instrumental instruction, theory, and ensemble playing.

City, state, and regional orchestras, bands, and choirs select members by audition. School music teachers can provide information and advice on preparing for these auditions. The frequency with which these groups rehearse and perform varies, depending in part on the distances students must travel. These ensembles offer students opportunities to meet and perform with talented young musicians from outside their schools and to work with different conductors. They frequently perform in small communities where professional orchestras do not travel, and their audiences are very receptive. The experiences of auditioning, rehearsing, and performing are valuable and enjoyable in themselves, and they also prepare students for similar experiences in college or in a career.

Some professional orchestras have youth symphonies that allow young musicians, selected by audition, to play under the direction of one of the orchestra's conductors and to meet the orchestra's musicians. Some of these orchestras also sponsor concerto competitions in which the first-place winner performs as a soloist with the youth orchestra. Youth orchestras are highly selective and offer challenging repertoire and standards. They are sometimes invited to perform out of state or even to travel abroad. Students who are sufficiently accomplished and dedicated to perform with these groups enjoy extraordinary opportunities.

Students may also wish to join or form small ensembles to perform classical chamber music, folk or rock music, or vocal music. Small ensembles may work independently (the norm for rock groups) or with a coach (as chamber groups often do). They provide wonderful musical experience, with young people selecting their own repertoire or writing their own music or arrangements, finding opportunities to perform before a variety of audiences, and learning during rehearsals how their fellow musicians hear, understand, and interpret the music. They must play or sing very well; because in a small group each performer is the only one playing a given part. For example, while in an orchestra a violinist or cellist is one of many and might rely on others to cover up mistakes, in a string quartet there is only one violist and one cellist, and each of the two violins has a separate part. Chamber music also gives performers the opportunity to add the chamber repertoire to their store of orchestral and solo pieces.

Playing in a small group also develops communication and social skills. Performers must learn to express their ideas and opinions, offer and accept criticism graciously, and persuade others to adopt their ideas and interpretations. Some of the communication skills are also musical skills, for the trio or quartet must play as a unit without verbal cues during a performance.

Organizational skills are essential, too, for these young people must develop their own rehearsal and performance schedules. Young musicians who play in these small groups may become musical entrepreneurs, actively soliciting opportunities to perform, setting and collecting fees, sharing income, and keeping track of earnings and expenses.

Whether students are hoping for a career in music, for the pleasure of amateur performance, or for a lifetime of attending concerts and listening to music, summer camps and programs are another way to develop musical skills, knowledge, and enjoyment. The young person whose school-year schedule is too busy to allow time for music beyond lessons and the school band can use the summer months to broaden musical horizons.

Summer programs can accommodate students at all levels, no matter what their interests and goals. Some are day programs and some are summer-long boarding camps. Some are designed for students at all levels of musical development, while others focus on the most accomplished students and are highly selective. Some specialize in only one instrument or family of instruments. Some offer all kinds of music, while others specialize in jazz or classical work. Some are free or inexpensive, while others are costly (these almost always offer scholarships). For beginners and younger students, camps can be great fun. They include a variety of musical experience, along with outdoor recreational activities. More experienced young musicians meet their peers and make friends from outside their communities. They may learn more difficult music than their high school ensembles can manage. Summer programs also include classes in theory, composition, and other subjects that high schools rarely offer. Students have an opportunity to measure their own musical accomplishments against those of a broader sample of young performers. They can work with new teachers during instrumental lessons, master classes, and ensemble playing. They may even develop some ideas about where they would like to study after high school if they find a wonderful teacher.

Whether it's at school, at camp, or in your garage, your child can gain a great deal of pleasure and achievement from playing music with others. As parents, you will enjoy hearing the group's progress and seeing your child grow musically and socially in good company.

chapter 9:

DECIDING WHEN TO STOP

Q: Do you think I should play and study the piano just because it is asked of me, and when I take no interest in it?

A: Most emphatically no! It would be a crime against yourself and against music.
—Josef Hofmann, *Piano Playing*

All good—and bad—things come to an end. At some point, you and your child will think about stopping music lessons. There are many reasons for quitting, including lack of progress, reaching the limit of one's musical potential, achieving the original goal, or frustration. In this chapter, we help you evaluate some of these reasons.

Josef Hoffman encouraged a student to end lessons when he lost interest because

> What little interest in music you may have left would be killed by a study that is distasteful to you, and this would be, therefore, bound to lead to failure. Leave this study to people who are sincerely interested in it. Thank heaven, there are still some of those, and there always will be some! Be sure, however, that you are really not interested and discriminate well between a lack of interest and a mere opposition to a perhaps too strenuous urging on the part of your relatives. My advice would be to quit the study for a time entirely; if, after a while, you feel a craving for music you will find the way to your instrument.

Even though this advice was given almost 100 years ago, the conflict remains unchanged. The question of whether to force a child to take music lessons or end music education is as painful as it was a century ago. To quit or not to quit? There are nearly as many ways to approach this question as there are students.

Imagine a child starting piano or violin lessons at a very young age. It is a novelty, and it is fun, like a new toy. The child loves playing with the big piano or the shiny violin and cooperates well at lessons. Everything looks and sounds promising. However, after a few months the toy becomes old; lessons and practicing take time away from other activities; the family is tired of listening to "Twinkle, Twinkle, Little Star" or "Chitty Chitty Bang Bang"; and tuition and instrument rental are beginning to seem expensive. The child senses the parents' (and perhaps the teacher's) frustration or displeasure and starts to avoid practicing at all costs, manipulating parents' doubts and impatience or throwing temper tantrums. Soon the child is making no progress at all, and parents feel justified in ending lessons. They often say, "He is not ready for lessons yet" and "We will try again later."

Will they try again? Most likely not, because the memory of the bad experience will linger. Can this situation be avoided? Probably. The parents of a young student should do a lot of homework. They should find the best teacher for their child, honestly evaluate their child's maturity, and make sure that they themselves are ready for a long, often bumpy and costly journey to the world of music. Following the suggestions in chapters 3 and 5 should help, but parents will also need to find ways to keep themselves and their children persisting through the rough places.

In music, all people are not created equal. Some are born with an exceptional propensity for music that manifests itself at an early age. Some have a good ear but lack in musicality or in other areas. Still others cannot carry a tune but would love to sing or play a musical instrument. The progress these different students make in studying music will naturally be very different. Some children progress quickly at the beginning of their studies and then slow down. Others start slowly, gradually accumulating information and understanding, and then suddenly blossom. It is therefore important for parents to be sensitive and patient. Do not monitor your child's progress in comparison with others. Instead, if you are concerned about the rate of progress, talk to the teacher. The music teacher is the only person who can evaluate your child's progress in relation to his or her natural ability and practice habits. (The teacher is also the only person who knows that the child who is progressing so much faster than yours is the product of three generations of talented musicians and practices three or more hours a day!)

Most children like music and music lessons but do not like practicing (see chapter 6). Poor practice habits or neglect of practice leads to a lack of progress, which is the primary cause for ending music lessons early on. Even the best students go through periods of frustration, slow progress, peer pressure, and a desire to spend more time on other activities; almost every student wants to quit lessons at some point—usually between the fifth and eighth grades.

Before you decide whether to allow your child to quit lessons, think back to the beginning. Whose idea was it to start lessons, yours or your child's? If it was originally your idea, your child was not enthusiastic, and lessons have not changed this, it may be time to stop. But if your child seems to have talent, you may want to persist. Doriot Dwyer, who was for many years the principal flutist with the Boston Symphony Orchestra, said that she hated the flute at first. Her mother was a flutist, and her parents "semi-forced me . . . to go to concerts and listen a great deal. And I thought I hated it, but I suppose I was really listening out of fascination. What I resented was their forcing me, so I didn't want to give them the satisfaction." Only when children are mature enough to discern their own likes and dislikes can they overcome such confusion of motives.

Were lessons just a whim or a fad—something to do this year, to be replaced next year by ballet? If so, and that has not changed, maybe it's time to call the dance academy. Did the idea stem from your own unfulfilled dream of playing an instrument? If so, maybe the wrong person is taking lessons. Was this something your child really wanted to do, but somehow you have both lost sight of why? The answers to these questions may provide some clues about the reasons behind your child's lack of interest, as well as some possible remedies.

Sometimes a child's wish to end music lessons has nothing to do with lessons. Just like the refusal to practice, the decision to quit may have more to do with friction in other aspects of your child's life. The eleven- or twelve-year-old who wants to stop lessons may really be saying, "I want to have more control over how I spend my time." Especially if music lessons were initiated by a parent, quitting may seem like a good way of asserting that claim to independence without confronting the issue directly. There are some ways to determine whether this is the underlying cause and, if so, to increase your child's sense of control without sacrificing music. You might begin by saying that you will allow your child to make that decision, but only after six months. Tell your child that she or he must deliver the news to the music teacher. In the meantime, detach yourself somewhat from lessons. Just drop your child off, instead of sitting in. Leave practicing problems up to your child and the teacher, without intervening. Look at other aspects of your child's life in which your control might be relaxed, for instance in setting bedtimes or the choice of television programs. In six months' time, your child may have forgotten about quitting lessons. In addition, you may find yourself with a more responsible preteenager who is ready to make sensible decisions.

The wish to quit lessons may also reflect another problem that children of this age must deal with: peer pressure. If the reason for stopping lessons is that other kids think music lessons are "uncool," this is as good a time as any to help your child think independently and assert independent judgment. Learning about other young musicians may provide some support and ammunition. A good book for this purpose is Amy Nathan's *The Young Musician's Survival Guide: Tips from Teens and Pros*. You may also have to allow your child to do some "cool" things to counter the uncoolness of music lessons, like wearing clothes or a hairstyle that you would otherwise not tolerate. Remember, hair grows back.

Did you or your child have a goal for lessons, and has the goal been accomplished? If so, maybe it is in fact time to move on. If not, why not? What were the obstacles? Was the goal realistic? Why exactly does your child want to stop lessons? If your child is frustrated because the music seems too difficult, even though he is practicing properly, talk to the teacher. Maybe it is time to slow down a bit. Is your child afraid of performing? Perhaps it would be a good idea to skip the next recital. If the teacher is unwilling to discuss the problems, or is inflexible about dealing with them, maybe it is time to look for a new teacher rather than giving up lessons. Perhaps a different instrument is the answer. Every possible solution should be explored before allowing the music in your child's life to die.

Some examples of children's experiences with lessons may help you to evaluate your child's motivations for ending lessons and to decide how to deal with them.

Peter

Peter started piano lessons at age five. He was a very bright little boy, but shy and quiet. He spoke almost in a whisper, and he played the piano at the same volume. By the fifth grade, he wanted to quit lessons because the recitals had become too painful for him. Peter's parents talked with his teacher, and she agreed not to require him to play in recitals until he was ready. She also decided to change the format of Peter's lessons. Appealing to his inquisitive mind, she focused on music theory, form, and history. Peter stopped worrying about recitals, started enjoying his lessons again, and resumed progress in his playing. Now a senior in high school, he plans to take music appreciation courses in college.

Ginny

After learning a long and technically difficult composition in a short time and performing it successfully at the annual recital, Ginny came to her lesson and, in her high-pitched voice, announced: "I decided to quit my piano lessons." Ginny, a sixth-grader, was one of her teacher's best students, the winner of a few competitions, and a bright, sweet girl. There had been no signs of any crisis, lack of progress, or problems with practicing. She was a student any teacher would treasure. Ginny's teacher concealed her shock and said, "Really? Why?" "I just don't want to do it any more."

Ginny's father, a physician, also studied piano with the same teacher and brought Ginny and her sister to their lessons. The teacher asked, "Did you talk to your father about this?"

"Yes," Ginny answered. "He said to talk to you."

"Well, Ginny," said the teacher, "if you quit, I quit too!" (In fact, that was exactly how the teacher felt.)

Now it was Ginny's turn to be shocked. "What do you mean?"

"Exactly what I said: If you quit, I quit. But before we do that, let's try something. I think that what happened to you is partly my fault. I put a lot of pressure on you last semester. You worked very hard, and now you are simply tired. Let's take it easy this summer but not quit."

Six months later, Ginny won another competition. She, her sister, and their father continued to enjoy their lessons and gave numerous solo and family recitals. The girls continued their study when they moved on to college, both choosing piano as their minor field while one majored in chemical engineering and the other in premedical studies. While Ginny was still in high school, she wrote about this incident for an English assignment. She described the pressure of self-induced competition with her older sister and father and told how she almost made the "mistake" of quitting. She recognized then, correctly, that music will always be an important part of her life.

Bill

Bill was an exceptionally talented student who started lessons at age four. When he was eight, he received a full national music scholarship. He was not the most diligent student, but his natural talent seemed to have no boundaries. However, even the most talented musicians have to practice. Talent requires discipline, but many talented students have problems accepting this fact. Bill was one of them. By the seventh grade he was torn between his teenage priorities and the love of his life: music. And then came the day when he asked, "What would you think if I took a break for a year?" He never used the word quit, but a year's break would have meant quitting. His teacher asked why he wanted a break: Was he tired? Having problems at school? "No, I just want to go out to the mall with my friends. I always have this 'practice' hanging over my head. I just want to be free."

After listening to all his "serious" reasons, the teacher said, "Okay. Go ahead. Quit. Just remember, you also lose your scholarship, and one year's break will put you behind in achieving your goal. However, if going to the mall is more important, then that is what you should do. I will wait for you to call me to confirm, because I need to know whether I can give your time slot to another student. You need to make your decision and call me tonight."

Two hours later he called and said, "I changed my mind. I am sorry. It was a moment of weakness." He stopped taking lessons only after graduating from high school but continues playing and composing. At this writing he is working on his second CD.

Nick

Nick came to his first lesson at the beginning of the new school year smiling and happily announced: "This is my last year! My mom said I can quit piano after the eighth grade, and I am in eighth grade now." Nick, the youngest of three siblings taking piano lessons from this teacher, is a sensitive and musical young man but not a very diligent student. His teacher looked at him very seriously and said, "I don't think I can let you quit this year, Nick. You still don't want to count when you play, and I can't let you go if you don't know how to count." "You can't do this!" exclaimed Nick, his eyes filled with tears. "You can't stop me!"

"Oh, yes I can," responded the teacher. "Remember, when your brother wanted to stop lessons, he had to continue for another year and a half because he had to master certain things before quitting?"

A few weeks later, the teacher made a remark about Nick's progress. "I can see, Nick, that you are really serious about quitting, because your counting and practicing have improved significantly. I may let you stop lessons at the end of this year after all."

"I am not really quitting music," said Nick. "I want to learn how to play the guitar now."

Coda

Unfortunately, not all stories have happy endings. Quite often children win the battle over music lessons and, in the long run, lose one of the most beautiful and rewarding parts of their lives. Most regret it later. Some adults never forgive their parents for letting them stop. (If they had accurate memories of how persistent and obnoxious they were in arguing their case, they might be more sympathetic toward their parents.) A few come back to music lessons, sometimes as adults with families and careers, and they struggle for every note they left behind in their childhood. (Noah Adams eloquently describes his adult struggles in *Piano Lessons*.)

Ideally, music lessons should continue until a child achieves a certain level of technical proficiency and comfort in playing an instrument; has sufficient knowledge and understanding of music theory; possesses reasonable sightreading skills; can approach a new composition without a teacher's help; and understands terminology, phrasing, articulation, timing, and rhythm. If your child can do all of those things and enjoys music, you have achieved the most important goal: you have a musically literate child. If your child also displays exceptional musical talent and love for music, and wants a career in music, he or she will continue developing these skills in college or a conservatory (see chapter 10). If your child, no matter how talented, chooses a career outside music, the time has been far from wasted. Your child can use all of that talent and accomplishment in college as an accompanist, as a member of an orchestra, band, or choir, and throughout life as an educated and appreciative listener.

When is quitting justified? Sometimes a student shows no interest in music despite all of the efforts and tricks of the trade the teacher has to offer. Even the best teacher cannot inspire an indifferent, undisciplined student who shows total disrespect for the teacher and for music. This behavior may be a protest against parents, or it may simply be a complete lack of musical sensitivity and of any desire to develop it. Often, when a child develops no interest and is impossible to teach, the teacher will initiate the break, offering to help the student find another teacher or another instrument. In extreme cases, the teacher may suggest that the student stop music lessons altogether.

Years ago, music lessons were a privilege of the very talented or the very rich. No respected music teacher would accept a student who did not have obvious, or even exceptional, musical ability—unless the teacher was starving and the student was wealthy. Nowadays, with music lessons easily accessible and affordable, they may not be given adequate respect. If you cancel music lessons frequently without any serious reason (such as illness or a real emergency) or allow your child to stop practicing regularly, you are sending the message that music lessons are not important, and you are not teaching responsible behavior or the importance of following through on commitments. This makes it more likely that your child will give up easily and want to quit lessons prematurely, wasting the time and money you have invested in music.

If you are very dedicated, never canceling lessons and making sure your child practices diligently, but your child still does not progress satisfactorily, do not give up without investigating the cause. Talk with the teacher, observe a lesson, and try to figure out what is missing. Maybe the personalities of your child and the teacher are incompatible. Their relationship, though friendly, may not generate the spark that will ignite your child's imagination. Perhaps the teacher's presentation is not interesting to your child, or too sophisticated. Or perhaps your child is daydreaming, and the teacher is discouraged by your child's lack of interest and progress. If any of these problems are present, they should be addressed before music lessons become a burden and a cause of family conflict, emotional problems, and even a lifelong dislike of music. If left untreated, such problems escalate, and the loser will be your child. Sometimes the best solution is to take a break from lessons and wait for the child to notice the loss of something valued.

Every family has its own dynamics, and everyone understands the importance of music education differently. The decision to end lessons really belongs to the parents. Only you know your own priorities and what is best for your child. But we do urge that, as you make this decision, you keep in mind the lasting value of understanding and appreciating music. With good teaching and support from parents, every child can develop a respectable level of skill in performing and a lifelong joy in listening. It is well worth a bit of patience and persistence.

If you decide lessons should end, find a tactful way to explain this to your child that leaves the door open for a return to music. Children should not feel like failures or misfits in such an important part of life. Even if—for whatever reason—they cannot master an instrument, all children can enjoy listening to music, attending concerts, and singing for fun. When they are older, they should recall the end of lessons without trauma or shame. Perhaps they will then want to try another instrument or at least find other ways to include music in their lives.

chapter 10:

CAREERS IN MUSIC

A musician is the hardest thing in the world to be.
If you want to do something easy, one musician
says, become a brain surgeon.
—Judith Kogan, *Nothing But the Best*

W hat is a career in music, and when and why does one decide to become a professional musician? Music is one profession you cannot suddenly choose after a few years of college if you have never had any musical training. You can decide to become a doctor, engineer, lawyer, teacher, or accountant in college or later, but not a musician. For the professional performer or teacher, musical training must begin in childhood.

Part of Life or Way of Life?

Being a professional musician is not just a career, but a way of life. And training alone—even the very best training, begun early—is not enough. A professional musician must have exceptional talent, a love for music, and tremendous determination. And, although musicians are generally underpaid and underappreciated (with the exception of a few lucky rock groups and superstars), many talented young people want to join this exclusive society. To serve in the Temple of the Goddess Music, the talented, dedicated, and selfless worshipers must sacrifice their childhood, youth, and quite often their personal lives. Famed pianist and teacher Gina Bachauer has said, "Music must always come first. Everything else must take second place. . . . It is an art that demands that you give and give."

If you are a proud parent of an exceptionally talented child who wants a career in music, you have to ask yourself and your child a lot of hard questions. There are many ways to apply one's musical talent: as a soloist, chamber music player, orchestra player, music teacher, conductor, composer, band leader, accompanist, music therapist, and more. Which career does your child have in mind?

Yehudi Menuhin, a child prodigy who had a long career as a renowned concert violinist, went on to found a music school in England for talented young people. His message to aspiring musicians, their parents, and their teachers is clear: "The important thing is to train young people so that they can take their place according to their talents. Opportunities dictate the need for soloists, orchestral players, quartet players or teachers. One boy has decided he wants to be a composer. It is also possible that some will go on to university and become ethnomusicologists."

The first dream of most people who consider a career in music is to become a soloist. The glamorous side of the performing artist's life has been the subject of numerous movies, such as *Rhapsody* and *The Competition*. In these movies, despite all odds (jealous competitors, injuries, and other disasters), a talented, sensitive, good-looking hero wins the most important international competition, which helps him to win the most beautiful girl, and all conflicts are resolved ten minutes before the end of the film. The lives of these musicians seem so exciting, surrounded by music, beautiful people, elegant receptions, international tours, and cascades of flowers! Musicians do what they love most—and get paid for it, too. What a life! But is it really that easy? And how many people become successful soloists? Although success stories dominate the movie screen, they are less common in real life. Screenwriters know that no one wants to see hours and hours of solitary practice, tears of frustration, broken dreams, jealousy, disappointment, backstabbing, physical and emotional exhaustion, or career-ending injuries. Very few musicians are destined to become stars.

The problem often is not a lack of talent. To become a soloist, in addition to exceptional talent, one must have qualities such as charisma, mastery of an instrument, an ability to express philosophical or spiritual values through music, iron determination and will power, strength of character, a well-rounded education, a thick skin, and . . . lots of luck. Alfred Brendel, one of the most successful concert pianists of our time, has said that parents should look for "certainly, talent; better yet, major talent. But talent in itself is not enough. There must also be such qualities as ambition and real persistence, which reveal themselves fairly early in the child's work. Without this it makes no sense to exploit the talent, even if it is very apparent."

In describing the life of Rachel Lee, then an eleven-year-old Juilliard student, journalist David Denby summarized the dilemma:

> Nurturing a prodigy is a high-risk game, not only for the parents but perhaps even for a renowned teacher. The odds against success are disagreeable to contemplate: only one out of every two hundred or so Juilliard music students will go on to have a stellar solo career. Imagine, if you can, that your child wanted to be a lawyer and began to think that no matter how

well she did in law school, no matter how many cases she tried and won, she would still be a failure if she was not appointed one of the nine justices of the Supreme Court. . . . Ambition like hers can kill, and yet there is no way to become a great musician without training muscles and instincts from an early age. Everyone knows this about prodigies, and everyone deplores the pressures they live under.

Professional performers, young or old, do not live normal nine-to-five lives. Music is their life. Their professional and personal lives are identical. Being a performer is one of the most difficult and physically and emotionally demanding jobs on earth, and often a very lonely one. "If he's lucky, he gets to live in airports and out of suitcases," writes Judith Kogan. "He goes onstage in strange cities to play his guts out for a thousand people he doesn't know, to return to an empty hotel room to rest up to catch a plane the next morning to another strange city to perform for another thousand people he doesn't know, to return to another empty hotel room. . . . Between his arrival at the airport and the rehearsal, he practices. Between the practice session and rehearsal, he prays. He prays the concert goes well, so he can repeat the cycle the next season." The competition is fierce and to stay on top is increasingly difficult. Many famous and seemingly successful musicians have turned to alcohol or drugs or experienced serious breakdowns at some point in their lives because of the tremendous stress of the profession. The stories of even the most talented and dedicated do not always have happy endings. Along with the other movies about classical musicians, we should also remember *Shine,* which dramatized the true story of a young Australian pianist who suffered a severe emotional breakdown.

At the same time, those who do succeed find extraordinary rewards. Arnold Steinhardt, first violinist of the Guarneri Quartet, has enjoyed success as a soloist, orchestra performer, and chamber music player. He has written not only about the pressures of competition and the boredom of touring but also about the enormous satisfaction of various kinds of performance. Against the tremendous satisfaction to the ego of winning a competition or completing a successful solo tour, he describes the emotional rewards of orchestra playing: "Being at an orchestra concert is a celebration of the aural palette, but being in the orchestra is like riding a giant wave. . . . the feeling was oceanic—what Sigmund Freud described in another context as 'a feeling of an indissoluble bond, of being one with the external world as a whole.'" In the end, he chose to play chamber music because "there is simply nothing better than playing string quartets and performing them in public." Remember, too, that very few instruments (really only piano, violin, flute, and cello) have enough of a solo repertoire to support a career exclusively as a soloist.

Lynn Harrell played the cello in a symphony orchestra before launching his career as a soloist. He notes that "the orchestral musician has to be able to do everything well. He must sight-read well. He must be able to play in any number of different styles and adjust to all kinds of colleagues and conductors. I think it is essential that a string player should spend some time in an orchestra or in playing chamber music." Flutist Julius Baker believes that "music is music. If you're a good player, you'll fit into chamber music, band, orchestra, or soloist. There is no such thing as specializing. A flutist who just plays solos is not developing into an all-around player." Parents and teachers of gifted children must make sure to expose them to the great variety of possible musical careers.

It is also possible that your child loves music and is devoted to an instrument, quite apart from thoughts of a career. Music may be a means of self-expression and development for an aspiring chemist, banker, or high school teacher. "Headstrong and idealistic, our young student has decided that success means finding something (in this case music) to which to relate in a personal way," wrote pianist and teacher Stewart Gordon. "It does not necessarily mean doing it better than the next guy (competition) or receiving approval for it. Growth means deepening love for this activity (music) and sharing it with others through more direct communication. It does not necessarily imply gaining a reputation as a hot shot performer or getting degrees. Fulfillment means becoming a master. It does not necessarily mean being able to earn a good living with this activity."

Dreams and Reality

Perhaps your child is a wunderkind, a star in the local music scene who wins all the competitions, who is the teacher's pride and the object of everyone's envy. You have a wall decorated with ribbons and trophies. And your child's imagination inflates with dreams of grandeur. As a parent, you have to act as ballast. You must keep your child's feet on the ground, preventing the balloon from flying too high and bursting too soon.

Musically gifted children are usually gifted in other areas, too. Parents need to determine what motivates their child, the reason she or he wants so badly to be a musician. Is it an all-consuming love for music? Fierce competitiveness? A need for praise and attention? Not one of these drives alone is enough to become a concert artist. And both competitiveness and the need for praise may be better served by other careers. As children enter their teenage years, their motivations may become clearer, and they may see other opportunities as more desirable than those available in the world of music. Parents can help them understand their goals and provide guidance.

Parents can also help their children be more realistic about exactly what is involved in succeeding beyond the local arena. Being a local star is only the first, very small step toward success on the international stage. Certainly by high school, but probably even earlier, the musically gifted child should be exposed to other very gifted young musicians, either through regional music activities and competitions or through selective summer programs that require auditions (see page 145). They may discover that their talent is great enough to perform well and accomplish much, but not great enough for a solo or orchestral career. Your child's teacher can help by offering an honest opinion of your child's abilities. If your child's teacher has no experience beyond the local community and cannot act as a mentor as your child enters a more competitive world, you will have to find a new teacher.

Parents whose children are serious about a musical career have an enormous responsibility. In addition to finding the very best teachers, parents must create an excellent working environment at home. Providing a good instrument, time to practice, and emotional support, accommodating a practice and competition schedule, offering transportation to lessons and performances—all of these needs place great demands on families. Some parents take extreme measures. To allow for more practice time, they homeschool their children or provide tutors. Some parents even move their families to cities where there are better musical opportunities. Before making such enormous commitments, and perhaps narrowing a child's opportunities prematurely, parents should be very sure that their children's dreams are both serious and realistic.

Parents also need to be sure they are not neglecting their children's nonmusical education. A good musician is not merely a technician, and mastery of an instrument and repertoire is not an adequate base for true musicianship. Fine musicians are well rounded, well read, and well educated. Pianist Gina Bachauer has reminded parents: "These children have to grow up, they have to go to school, they have to learn languages. An artist, years ago, who played the piano very well was sometimes a complete idiot apart from piano-playing. It's not in fashion anymore to be uninformed and poorly educated. Today, an artist is a human being with whom everybody wants to discuss not only music, but painting, sculpture, literature, everything. A young man or woman today must be completely ready for all of this."

Cellist Yo-Yo Ma already had a flourishing concert career when he was in his teens, but at seventeen he decided to apply to Harvard. Violinst Isaac Stern, who devoted his own youth to musical study and did not attend college, described Ma's choice as "remarkable": "He could have devoted all his time to preparing pieces for concerts and competitions, but he took the unusual step of deciding to become a person." As adults, musicians whose education was limited to their instruments from a very early age feel acutely the absence of a liberal education. They often read voraciously to make up for what they missed. Being well educated contributes to musicality, but it also provides much needed balance in the musician's life.

The question of education becomes most important when the young musician makes a decision about what to do after high school. What is the best choice: to pursue a musical career immediately, attend a conservatory, or attend a liberal arts college or university? Violinist Jane Bowyer Stewart, who chose Yale University over a conservatory, has described the effect of that choice on her life and career:

> Every time I research and compose program notes, I use skills developed in college. As I seek to create original performances, I call upon the critical thinking emphasized in my humanities courses. . . . My literature background gives me a familiarity with composers' inspirational sources and keeps the music fresh for me. My fascination with languages helps me enjoy deciphering obscure musical instructions and libretti,

and the contemporary repertoire taxes all my math skills. . . .
I might have risen to a finer orchestra or have been a finer violinist had I gone the conservatory route, but having developed
a host of other interests gives me perspective when my trills are
too slow or the piccolo is too loud.

We advise students to seek out either a conservatory that offers an excellent curriculum in both music and the liberal arts or a college that accom-
modates the needs of performers by making it easy to study with excellent
music teachers. Some conservatories and liberal arts colleges have joint
programs. The aspiring musician should investigate a variety of options
and visit as many campuses as possible before deciding where to apply and
audition.

We do not believe that most young people are ready to launch a
career immediately after high school. No matter how great their talent
and accomplishment, they are not ready to travel independently, make
career decisions, or deal with the public. Certainly there are a handful of
exceptions, young people who have begun concert careers in their teens
and continued as successful musicians into adulthood. These are rare, and
they have had extraordinary adult support from parents, teachers, and
sometimes patrons. More commonly, child prodigies disappear from the
concert world as young adults, for a variety of reasons, and they are ill
prepared for any other kind of life.

Finally, parents and children need to talk seriously about what to do
if a solo career is not possible. Will your child be happy as an orchestra
performer, a member of a chamber group, or a teacher? If the answer is
no, then the child should plan for another career—not only because the
odds of success are small but also because this answer suggests that it is
not the music that is the attraction but the applause. Someone who truly
loves music will always find a way to include it in his or her life, no
matter what career occupies the day. Federal Reserve Board chair Alan
Greenspan studied clarinet at the Juilliard School, physicist Albert
Einstein played the violin, National Security Advisor Condoleezza Rice
trained to be a concert pianist, and physician Albert Schweitzer was an
accomplished organist. Each continued as an enthusiastic amateur while
enjoying a successful nonmusical career. There is even a rock band of
writers that includes "horror king" Stephen King, humorist Dave Barry,

and novelists Amy Tan and Barbara Kingsolver. A doctor, lawyer, engineer, or scientist can also be a happy musician, but an unhappy musician will be just that.

Stewart Gordon has pointed out that the effort and sacrifice that a young person invests in music is never wasted: "Should the years ahead produce simply an ardent amateur musician, then this person's life will still have been immeasurably enriched by music. Study may continue, buying concert tickets and collecting recordings may be a way of life, and this music fan will probably make some effort to pass the joy of music on to his or her children. Then this love affair with the music is one which is of benefit to all parties." The great pianist Ignace Paderewski said, "Far too many students study music with the view to becoming great virtuosi. Music should be studied for itself. The intellectual drill which the study of music gives is of great value—there is nothing that will take its place. And, in addition, the study of music results in almost limitless gratification in later life in the understanding of great musical masterpieces."

Beyond the Concert Stage

Most professional musicians learn to balance their lives as solo performers, teachers, chamber group players, and accompanists. They do this not only to earn a better living but to enrich their experience and broaden their musicianship. The most powerful musical personality is rooted deeply in all facets of the art.

Ninety-five percent of professional musicians depend on teaching as the main source of their professional income. Yet, if you ask a young music student whether he or she wants to teach, most likely you will get a frowning "Oh, no. I can't see myself sitting all day correcting wrong notes and fingers!" Music teachers are often portrayed as second-class citizens in the republic of music, losers who did not make it as performers. (They share this lack of respect with teachers of other subjects: "Those who can, do; those who can't, teach.") These belittling remarks may initially turn a few young, ambitious musicians from teaching careers. However, many of them will eventually realize that a performing career is not in their stars, that performing alone will not feed them and their families, or that the stresses of performance on their minds, bodies, and families are not worth the applause. Others find that teaching contributes to their general musical abilities. Paula Robison has said, teaching "has helped me to be able to express my musical ideas better." Teaching may then become the most rewarding and fulfilling part of their professional lives. As pianist Leon Fleisher notes: "I think, in a sense, that teaching is one step beyond performing. Teaching entails more responsibility. There's a greater obligation in teaching than in being a very great and successful performer today, because . . . if you're a teacher, and you pass on nonsense, then I think you commit a grave sin."

Teaching provides a lot of flexibility and freedom. If you are an aspiring composer working on your first immortal symphony, teaching will be a better-paying, more challenging, and more rewarding way to put bread on the table than waiting on tables. While a young person may be moved to study music by witnessing a brilliant concert performance, it is the work of the music teacher, week after week, that keeps that inspiration alive, nurtures it, and gives the student the opportunity to participate in the world of music.

In every profession, the best of the best teach. They transfer their experience, their knowledge, and their expertise from one generation to the next. A music teacher is privileged not only to provide knowledge about music and an instrument but to play an important role in the student's development as a human being, to influence and shape a young person's thinking. Teachers, by their example, should show aspiring musicians that teaching is a desirable career. But parents, too, should send a message to the child that, if a performing career is not available or adequate, teaching is an equally important, rewarding, and prestigious way to share musical talent with others.

chapter 11:

THE HARMONIOUS CHILD FROM BIRTH TO COLLEGE

One of the many unique characteristics of music and art is that they are appealing and accessible on many levels. The child can often enjoy them on his childlike level (which may not, by the way, always be a completely simple one) and the adult can enjoy them on his level.

—Donald Elliott and Clinton Arrowood,
Alligators and Music

Parents can begin to make music and music lessons a part of their child's development at any time from pregnancy through high school. After that, your child will probably make decisions independently about learning an instrument, studying music theory or history, or learning about different kinds of music. Music education includes many kinds of activities: listening, moving, singing, reading, and playing. Which activities are most appropriate for children of different ages?

Pregnancy

Music has a soothing and healing effect, so it makes sense to surround yourself with music that you enjoy when you are expecting. At some point during pregnancy, your unborn child will begin to join you in listening. Any music that you like will do, but there are actually recordings designed especially for this purpose, including one called *Ultra Sound*, listed in "For Further Information."

When you are in the last trimester of pregnancy, you may discover that music affects your baby's level of activity. If you pay attention to the kinds of music that soothe your baby and the kinds that inspire soccer practice, you can take advantage of that knowledge. Once your baby is born, he or she will respond to the music the same way. Similarly, rhythmic motion that calms your baby before birth will have the same effect on your newborn. Some musicians even claim that their babies recognize the music that they were practicing during pregnancy!

From Birth to Three

The youngest children can listen and move to music. They will also enjoy hearing their parents read poetry and rhythmic prose. There are even some classes appropriate for toddlers.

Listening

Children can listen to music from the moment they are born. Babies quickly learn to recognize their parents' speaking voices (they may recognize them before they are born, in fact), and they can also learn their singing voices. Being sung to is an important part of ear training. It helps your child develop a sense of melody and rhythm, as well as a love of music and musical expression. Perhaps babies with a very good ear might object to a parent's off-key singing, but most will not mind how well you perform. Nursery rhymes, lullabies, nonsense songs, or anything you like will make them happy. You can also play recorded songs, beginning with vocal music with or without accompaniment. When babies are a few months old—around the time they sleep through the night and seem to be focusing more on their surroundings—you can add recorded instrumental music or your own playing.

Of course, you can always play whatever kinds of music you usually listen to. The sounds will quickly become familiar to your baby. But it is probably a good idea to avoid anything very loud or lively at naptime. You may also find that your baby finds music distracting at mealtimes. This is a sign that the baby notices the music, which is good, but if eating is the main task, it might be better to hold the entertainment until the meal is over. Some parents, though, invent an eating song that accompanies meals.

Toddlers will listen happily to many kinds of music, and they will begin to sing as they become more verbal. There is an enormous amount of recorded music for children—everything from nursery rhymes to nonsense songs to jazz and classics selected for youngsters. Provide a variety of recorded music for your child. Some recordings will quickly become favorites, but always add something new from time to time.

If you are not sure how to approach the listening process and are not familiar with classical music, the best way to start is with "program music"—music that has a story—such as Sergei Prokofiev's *Peter and the Wolf*, Paul Dukas's *The Sorcerer's Apprentice*, Modest Moussorgsky's *Pictures at an Exhibition*, or orchestral arrangements of ballets and operas with familiar stories, such as Peter Ilich Tchaikovsky's *The Nutcracker* or Englebert Humperdinck's *Hansel and Gretel*. Many of these pieces are the subject of picture books that you can read to your child. As you listen to the music, you and your child can try to identify the characters and the events in the musical themes. When listening to music with abstract names and no apparent story, such as a symphony or concerto, you and your child might want to make up your own story. Another trick that music students use to remember pieces for exams might also come in handy: setting words to the opening theme. For example, the first movement of

Mozart's *Symphony No. 40* has been known to generations of music students as "It's a bird, it's a plane, it's a Mozart."

Listening to poetry also helps develop a child's sense of rhythm. Children love poems with a pronounced meter, and you can exaggerate the accents slightly. Nursery rhymes are the usual first choice, but there are many, many volumes of poetry for children of all ages.

Moving

Babies respond well to rhythmic motion—rocking chairs, swings, and the like. This movement is useful in itself, but you can also add music to it. Rock in time to a lullaby, swing in time to nursery rhymes, and so on. Move your baby's arms and legs in time to music or to a rhythmic poem, and clap with older babies. Once children learn to stand and walk, they can also begin to dance and march to music on their own or with a parent. Even a baby who can only sit up can sway in time to music—and probably will do so with little or no urging.

To add to the fun and musical benefits of movement, buy or make bands with bells sewn on them that fasten to the toddler's ankles or wrists with Velcro. (Make sure the bells are securely fastened, and if your baby chews on them, save them until she or he is older.) These provide an aural feedback from the child's motion. Another alternative is easy-to-grip toys with bells. Toddlers can also use maracas or easy-to-hold rattles.

Clapping is another rhythmic activity that babies can do, at first with help. Patty-cake and other clapping games are always good, and you can add clapping to whatever songs you sing to your baby. It's good for coordination as well as fun. Children who are dancing and marching will probably add clapping and other ways of making noise. Toddlers may want to enhance clapping by using blocks, pot lids, or other percussion "instruments."

As your child gets older and more verbal, talk about music. Is this music happy or sad? What makes you happy? What makes you sad? Why do you suppose the music is sad? Can you tell me a story about it? Maybe we can draw a picture. This develops sensitivity to emotions as well as to music and encourages your child's imaginative growth.

Reading

It is essential and fun to read to children. It promotes intellectual development, awakens an interest in books and reading, and prepares children to read on their own. It also provides opportunities for parents and children to spend quiet time together and to talk about what they read. Even infants enjoy having stories read to them and will include cloth and board books among their favorite toys. Many books for toddlers are rhythmic or call attention to sound as well as meaning. We have already mentioned poetry, but books designed to prepare children to read also emphasize sound. The many books by Dr. Seuss are a good example, with their strong rhythm, rhymes, and repeated sounds, words, and syllables. Reading these books to your child is important for verbal development, but it also benefits your child musically. You might also want to add some books about music. "For Further Information" includes a list of picture books about music that are suitable for toddlers.

Classes

Music classes for toddlers should emphasize the same activities that you engage in at home: listening, dancing, and rhythmic movement. They should also offer children a variety of ways of making sounds—lots of percussion instruments, including bells, chimes, and other instruments that have pitch. Toddlers are not ready for music theory or flashcards. And do not worry about being "late" if you do not enroll your child in formal lessons. Listening and making music at home are more important at this age than classes.

Child Care

If your toddler is in day care, look for a program that includes the activities we have suggested for home. When you visit, you should hear children singing and being sung to, being read to, dancing, playing with toys that make noise, and playing games that include clapping and motion.

From Three to Six

Once children are walking, talking, and toilet trained, they can participate in a greater variety of musical activities at home, in classes, and in preschool. Some may even be ready to learn an instrument.

Listening

Preschoolers will enjoy listening to the same sorts of music they liked as toddlers, but at this age they can listen more actively. They can sing along with better intonation and rhythm (though they are still likely to mangle the words), and they can play song games like "The Wheels on the Bus," where they sing and perform motions. They can clap along with songs to master rhythm, or use homemade or real percussion instruments. They may also begin to recognize the sounds of the more distinctive instruments, with a little help from *Peter and the Wolf.*

You can count to music with your child when you listen to music with a clear beat. Before you know it, your child will recognize waltzes and marches. If a child begins lessons on an instrument, you can play recordings of solo pieces for the instrument for inspiration and education. It helps children to know what the instrument is supposed to sound like. In some teaching methods, including Suzuki, children listen to tapes of the pieces they are learning.

Moving

Preschoolers can learn more sophisticated dance steps and participate in more advanced eurythmics classes. They can also make up stories to music and dance or act out the stories.

Reading

Picture books are still appropriate for children of this age, and favorites will emerge. The reading readiness books, like those by Dr. Seuss, are definitely helpful both for reading and for developing a sense of rhythm and sound. If your child is listening to or playing music by famous composers, he or she may enjoy the biographies written for young children.

Classes

More advanced versions of the same sorts of classes that are appropriate for toddlers are good for preschoolers. In addition, they can be introduced to the sounds and appearances of various instruments and can learn a variety of rhythms. They can also sing in a more organized fashion and work on carrying a tune and following a conductor to sing in a group.

Preschool

Look for a preschool that offers singing, dancing, and rhythmic movement as well as training specifically in music. Children in this age group can learn to play percussion instruments, bells, and xylophones. Some preschools may teach with Orff instruments, specially designed to help small children master the elements of music, or may use one of several music-education programs designed for preschoolers.

Lessons

Some preschool children are ready for lessons on an instrument, but only if you find an excellent teacher who has experience with such young students and who feels that your child is ready. (Chapters 3 and 5 discuss evaluating readiness and finding a teacher.) Lessons for children this age should be no longer than half an hour, once a week. Whether your child will learn to play by ear or to read music depends on the teacher's training and on what she or he thinks will work best for your child. If your child does begin lessons this early, make sure your goals and evaluation of his or her musical abilities are realistic. At this age, lessons should be fun, and technical progress is a minor concern.

Parents should attend the lessons and pay close attention to the teacher's instructions. It may even be a good idea to take notes. This is a good opportunity to watch your child's interaction with the teacher, not only to make sure that you have made the right choice but also to get to know your child's learning style. If your attendance disrupts the lesson (e.g., if your child shows off for you or is distracted by your presence), you can sit outside the room and ask the teacher for a summary of instructions at the end of the lesson.

Practicing

Preschoolers will need help with practicing (see chapter 6). Parents should set the time for practicing, remind the child when it is time, and listen to be sure that the child is playing the right pieces, and following the teacher's instructions. Do not leap at every wrong note, but do correct repeated errors. (Even if you do not play an instrument, you will recognize mistakes in the kinds of pieces that preschoolers play.)

Preschoolers may spend part of their practice time just fooling around with the instrument. This is okay: they are becoming comfortable with the instrument, experimenting, and perhaps making early attempts at composing. As long as they are also accomplishing what they are supposed to, let them have fun.

Performing

Your child's teacher will hold recitals of some kind. For preschoolers, some teachers hold monthly informal recitals where a small group of children play for one another and for their parents. Others hold one or two more formal recitals each year. Preschoolers usually enjoy these events and are rarely nervous. You can also hold informal recitals at home if your child wants to perform for friends or family. Do not force (or bribe) a preschooler to perform, though.

Elementary School Children (Six to Ten)

Children in elementary school can begin more formal music training, but it is important to continue to listen to music at home, attend performances, and have fun.

Listening

Parents should make sure that elementary school children have access to a variety of good music either on the radio or on recordings. With help, children this age can learn something about pieces they enjoy as well as the performer and the composer by consulting the liner notes on a recording or by looking in a reference book. Liner notes are often far too complex for children (and for adults lacking a fair amount of music education), but you can always find a few relevant and interesting facts. You can also use listening as an opportunity for creative play. Children can make up stories, dance, paint, or draw to music.

Talk to your child about favorite pieces. These discussions can be more sophisticated than the ones you had when your child was a toddler. What kind of mood does the music create? (Children can begin to move beyond "happy" and "sad.") What instruments can you hear? Is it fast or slow, loud or soft? What happens when the tempo or dynamics change? What does the music make you think of? Does this piece sound like any others you know? This last question may yield some interesting answers. Children may say that one loud piece sounds like another, or that one waltz sounds like another, or they may make completely different connections.

By the end of elementary school, children who are studying music may begin to recognize certain composers and types of pieces (e.g., symphonies or piano concertos).

Variety is important but so is repeated listening. This usually happens with no effort on the parents' part because children will play favorite pieces over and over. By listening to a piece frequently, children are subconsciously learning about harmony, melody, tempo, and rhythm.

Elementary school children are old enough to attend concerts with their parents. Look for special children's performances that select music likely to appeal to young people, performed in the afternoon, and not too long. Be sure to explain good concert manners to your child before attending.

Moving

In elementary school, children learn circle and other dances, and they may become much more interested in dancing and rhythmic movement. Dance lessons are a good idea if your child is interested and has time. They improve coordination and posture, and they add a dimension to your child's appreciation of music.

Reading

Your child is now learning to read independently, but don't stop reading aloud! You can read books that are at a level your child cannot manage yet. These are generally more interesting to you and your child, and they also introduce children to more sophisticated sentence structure, punctuation, and vocabulary. Children this age often want to watch the page as you read, which is even more helpful. There are lots of books about music, performers, and composers for children ages six to ten that you can include in your reading. Also, be sure to allow your child to read to you. This makes children more fluent, confident readers and gives them a chance to be proud of their accomplishments.

Classes

Children in elementary school can learn some music theory, music history, sight-singing, and music appreciation. If your child is not ready for instrumental lessons or is not interested in playing an instrument, classes such as these provide a good way to include music in your child's education. A community center or nearby music school or college is a good place to look.

School

Ask your child's teacher about the school's music program. If there is none, talk to the principal (and, if necessary, the school board) about changing this. If there is no program at all, a group of parents can get together and arrange field trips to youth concerts or visits by musicians to the school. You can put together a list of free or inexpensive musical events and arrange carpools. Talk to the teacher about having a talent show where children can share their own singing, playing, or dancing.

Lessons

By the age of seven or eight, most children can benefit from music lessons. We have talked in chapters 4 and 5 about choosing an instrument and a teacher. But children who do not take private lessons can still learn an instrument through group lessons in school or by joining a school music ensemble. Singing in a children's choir is another excellent way to learn about and enjoy music.

Practicing

Elementary school children need some encouragement and supervision when they are practicing, but less than preschoolers. A beginner of any age needs help developing good practice habits, but once they are established you can step back a bit. Each child is different, and some will want or need help. Others may be able to work on their own most of the time. Consult chapter 6 for guidance.

Performing

If your child is taking music lessons, he or she will have opportunities to play in recitals and competitions. Chapter 7 contains information about such performances. If your child is not interested in performing, don't worry about it. Some children become more outgoing as they get older, and they may then wish to enter competitions. Others will never want to compete musically. Ultimately, most people play for their own enjoyment, and if your child gets pleasure from playing, that is more than enough.

Middle School and Junior High (Ten to Thirteen)

Preteenagers begin to have definite opinions about many things, including music. Activities with their peers become important, and you can find ways to include music among these. Children also want some independence in decision making, which affects lessons and practicing.

Listening

In middle school, children are developing their own tastes in music. Continue to offer them all kinds of music. By now, children are definitely ready to attend concerts. Don't forget the many free performances often available in many cities, including the regional and state youth orchestras, bands, and choirs. Seeing performances by children just a few years older may pique your child's interest in playing a first or second instrument and joining a school ensemble now or in high school.

Moving

Dance lessons are still a good idea for junior high students, especially if they feel they need help with coordination and posture.

Reading

In junior high, students begin to write short research papers and learn to use the library and Internet resources. You can encourage your child to choose musical subjects for papers where this is appropriate, or to just look up composers, genres, or instruments for fun.

Classes

Summer music programs are a good idea for junior high students. "For Further Information" offers suggestions about finding the right camp or institute for your child.

School

The big change in junior high is the opportunity to join a band, choir, or orchestra. Encourage your child to do this and take a look at the suggestions in chapter 6. However, there is one junior high phenomenon that you should be aware of. Some children this age, especially boys, do not want their peers to know that they can play an instrument. They happily attend lessons, play in recitals, and even win competitions, but they tell no one at school. It is almost as though they belong to a secret cult or elite society. This is a strange mix of pride and embarrassment. They are proud of their accomplishments but worry that they are "uncool." This is often a special problem for piano students, because students who play other instruments can be part of the band or orchestra, thereby joining an "acceptable" school group.

If your child would really like to let people know about his or her musical accomplishments, talk to the music teacher about opportunities to perform in school, play a videotape of a performance, or exhibit awards and medals. Young musicians who work hard deserve to have their accomplishments recognized, just like their peers who excel in sports or geography bees. However, if your child really prefers to keep music a private matter, respect those wishes. This will probably change in high school, when young people learn to respect a greater variety of accomplishments.

Lessons

If your child has not started lessons, this is a good time to begin almost any instrument. Children who have been studying piano may wish to take up a second instrument to join a band or orchestra. You can discuss with your child's teacher whether you should continue to sit in on lessons. It may be time to step back a little.

Practicing

Junior high is the time for children to begin taking responsibility for practicing, but it is also a time when other demands and other temptations are strong. Children at this age need their parents' support and encouragement to continue with lessons and to find the time to practice. They do not need supervision during practice.

Performing

Children may wish to continue or to begin entering competitions. In junior high, competition becomes much more common: there are spelling bees, geography bees, competitive sports, and all sorts of activities that allow children to start accumulating ribbons and trophies. If your child wishes to compete, discuss this with the music teacher and find the most appropriate opportunities. Children may also want to participate in school talent shows or just play informally for friends.

For many children, junior high is a very trying emotional time. Many are uncomfortable in their rapidly changing bodies, and they become very self-conscious. If they do not want to perform, do not force the issue.

High School

Teenagers need some independence to develop a sense of responsibility. They should be making their own decisions about what music to listen to and about their level of commitment to lessons. Parents still need to be involved, though, in helping their teenagers with important choices.

Listening

High school students decide for themselves what music to listen to, and they may begin their own collections of recordings. Be sure to continue to talk to your children about their choices of music and try to understand what they are listening for and what they enjoy.

Reading

High school students may not have time to read much beyond their school assignments, but they can continue to read about music and musicians if they wish.

Classes

Summer music camps and programs are a good idea for teenagers (see page 145). Students considering a career in music should apply to some of the selective national programs as a way to evaluate their own abilities on a larger stage than their hometown.

School

High school is prime time for band, choir, and orchestra. Provide logistical support to help your child take advantage of these opportunities (see chapter 8). If the school also offers music history, theory, or appreciation, encourage your child to find time for it in his or her schedule. During high school, time pressures can become even more intense, especially for students who participate in extracurricular activities. If these pressures make your child consider dropping music lessons, talk seriously about priorities and the reasons for the decision. The discussion in chapter 9 may be helpful. If your child decides to continue lessons, offer help with time management.

Lessons

Teenagers should attend their lessons on their own and work as independently as possible. If you drive your child to lessons, it's probably a good idea to find a nearby place to have coffee rather than sitting in. If your child's music teacher needs to talk with you, this can be done at the beginning or end of the lesson.

More advanced students may need longer lessons: an hour once a week instead of half an hour is typical, but two hours a week is not unheard of. If your child is willing to make this kind of time commitment (including extra practicing) and would benefit from additional lesson time—and if you can afford it—consider this option.

Practicing

Teenagers should take complete responsibility for their practicing and for the consequences of not practicing. Parents should intervene only if the child or teacher asks.

Performing

High school students will be performing in school ensembles and may also wish to compete for chairs in regional, state, and other honors ensembles. They will play in class recitals and may also wish to enter competitions. At this age, there are some very talented and dedicated young musicians competing, and it is difficult to win medals without a lot of work. Encourage your child if she or he wishes to compete and emphasize the value of the experience rather than the medals.

Moving On

During high school, your child will be making a number of important decisions, with your help. An interest in music affects some of these decisions. For example, if your child wants to continue with music lessons, the availability of instruction will affect the choice of college. High school students may begin to investigate the possibilities of a career in music (see chapter 10). If they are serious about this possibility, then they may want to consider a conservatory. At a minimum, they will want to make sure that they can easily take lessons from an excellent teacher. Students who plan to end their music lessons at high school may still want to make sure the college has a good program in music history and theory. They may also want to join a college band, orchestra, choir, or chamber group. Once they have left home, though, decisions about music are their own. If you have helped them lay a firm foundation and have awakened their love of music, you need not worry that they will abandon it.

Return on Your Investment

In just a few pages, we have taken you through eighteen years of music and growing up. In real life it doesn't go quite that fast, but it passes much more quickly than you might imagine. Enjoy your children and the music they listen to and play. The investment of time, money, and effort will be returned many times over.

glossary

Below are short definitions of musical terms used throughout this book as well as terms that are part of the early years of musical study. Terms within definitions that are in **boldface** are defined separately in the glossary. Recommendations for a musical dictionary are provided on page 144 ("For Further Information").

accompaniment: The musical background for a principal part, performed by a full orchestra or a single performer such as a pianist.

accompanist: The person, usually a pianist or harpsichordist, who plays the accompaniment for a solo instrumentalist or vocalist.

adagio: (1) As a **tempo** marking, slow, leisurely; (2) a composition written in a slow tempo, often the second movement of a **sonata, concerto,** or **symphony**.

allegretto: (1) As a **tempo** marking, lively, moderately fast (faster than **andante** but slower than **allegro**); (2) a short piece to be played at a lively speed.

allegro: (1) As a **tempo** marking, lively, rapid, cheerful, brisk; (2) a movement of a composition in this tempo, often the first or last in a piece.

alto: High; the low voice of females and boys, also called contralto, which is higher than the voices of adult male singers.

andante: At a moderate pace; literally, walking.

andantino: A word with contrary meanings—either a little slower or a little faster than **andante**.

aria: An air, song, tone, or melody, used in several ways: (1) a fully developed theme; (2) a tranquil and richly harmonized second section of a piece; (3) a repetition of a first section with more elaborate ornamentation; (4) a solo in an opera.

arpeggio: A broken **chord**, one with the notes played in even succession instead of all at once, in imitation of the way a chord is played on a harp.

articulation: The way the performers join notes to one another and a principal component of **phrasing**.

bass: (1) The lowest tone in a **chord** or the lowest part in a composition (e.g., the left hand in a piano composition, or the cello in a string **quartet**); (2) the lowest male voice; (3) a singer with a bass voice; (4) the lowest of the string instruments, often called a double bass or contrabass.

bass clef: F **clef**, placed on the fourth line of the **staff**.

bridge: The piece of wood over which the strings of violins, violas, cellos, and basses are stretched and which transmits vibrations to the body of the instrument.

chair: A musician's position in a section of the band or orchestra. The first chair of the first violin section is called the concertmaster or concertmistress.

chamber music: Music written to be performed in a home or small hall, in which there is usually only one player for each part. Chamber music may be vocal or instrumental.

chord: (1) Two or more tones sounding together; (2) a string.

chromatic scale: The succession of halftones, for example, C, C sharp, D, D sharp, E, F, and so on.

clef: A sign written at the beginning of each **staff** that designates the **pitches** of the lines and spaces.

coda: A tail; thus, the concluding bars of a piece of music.

con: Italian for *with*. For example, *con moto* means "with motion" and *con anima* means "with animation."

concert: A musical performance.

concerto: A long composition for a solo instrument and orchestra.

conservatory: A school that provides practical and theoretical musical instruction. Originally, in Italy, a *conservatorio* was an orphanage where children were given academic and musical training.

counting: Using numbers, aloud or silently, to regulate the duration of the notes.

crescendo: Gradually increasing in loudness.

Dalcroze method: Music education that teaches **rhythm** through movement but also **solfège** and keyboard improvisation, developed by Swiss composer Jacques Dalcroze (1865–1950).

diminuendo: Gradually decreasing in loudness.

dolce: Sweetly, softly.

duet: A composition for two performers, for example, two pianists, a pianist and violinist, or a guitarist and vocalist.

dynamics: The changes in loudness or softness of musical tones.

ecossaise: A dance or tune in Scottish style.

embouchure: (1) The mouthpiece of a woodwind or brass instrument; (2) the placement of the lips and tongue in playing such an instrument.

étude: A study; a composition designed to help students develop their technique. Some are performed as recital and concert pieces.

exercise: A short piece designed to help the student overcome a special technical difficulty, or a short study in composition.

fermata: (⌒) The prolongation of a note or rest at the performer's discretion.

finale: The last piece or **movement** of a **symphony** or **sonata**.

fingering: (1) The way fingers are placed on the keys, strings, or holes of an instrument; (2) the numbers printed in the music indicating which fingers the performer is to use; for piano, each thumb is 1.

flat: The character, ♭, which lowers the pitch of the following note by a half **tone**.

forte: Loud, strong; abbreviated *f*.

fortissimo: Very loud, abbreviated *ff*.

fret: A narrow piece of wood, metal, or ivory that runs across the fingerboard of a guitar or similar instrument.

harmony: The study of **chords** and their progression.

interval: The difference in **pitch** or distance between two **notes**, defined by the number of lines and spaces on the **staff** or the number of letter names it contains. For example, C and E are a third (C, D, E = 1, 2, 3)

intonation: The production of **tone** in vocal or instrumental music; also, playing in tune.

Juilliard: The Juilliard School, a leading arts **conservatory** located in New York City, often used as a shorthand for the highly selective conservatories such as the Curtis Institute, Peabody Conservatory, Oberlin Conservatory, and Eastman School of Music.

key: (1) The series of **tones** that form any **major** or **minor scale** based on a key note and the relations of other tones to it; (2) the mechanical part of the piano (or other instrument that uses levers) that the finger presses to make a sound.

key signature: The **sharps** or **flats** on the **staff** that indicate the **key** in which the following section of the piece is written.

Kodály method: Music education based on singing, emphasizing the folk music of a child's culture, that teaches students to read and write music, sing, improvise, and compose; developed by Hungarian composer and teacher Zoltan Kodály (1882–1967).

largo: Very slow.

legato: Played or sung smoothly and evenly; connected.

leggiero: Lightly.

lento: Slow.

libretto: The words of an opera or other vocal work. The author is called a librettist.

major: Contrasted with **minor**; the greater form of an **interval** or **mode**. A major **scale** has a different pattern of whole and half tones than a minor scale.

ma non troppo: Italian for "but not too," for example, *allegro ma non troppo* means rapidly but not too fast.

march: A composition exhibiting a regular **rhythm** alternating accented and unaccented beats, in 4/4 time, suitable for marching.

measure: The notes and rests between two vertical ("bar") lines that is the unit of meter in a composition. Each measure has the same number of beats and a regular accent.

melody: A series of musical tones arranged by **pitch** and duration, the "tune."

metronome: A device that ticks or flashes at a speed set by the musician. It is used to show the performer the speed at which a piece is to be played and to provide a regular beat. The setting for the metronome is indicated on the music with a note followed by an equal sign and the speed.

minor: A lesser **interval, mode**, or type of **scale**; contrasted with **major**.

minuet: A dance form, originally French, with three beats to a measure, typically more stately than a **waltz**. It usually consists of a first section followed by a second section called a **trio** and then a repeat of the first section.

mode: A series of **intervals** forming a **scale**, either **major** or **minor**.

moderato: at a moderate speed. Sometimes combined with another indication of **tempo**, for example, *allegro moderato,* moderately fast.

molto: Very.

movement: A section of a composition.

natural: The character, ♮, which cancels a **sharp** or **flat**.

note: A symbol that represents the duration and **pitch** of a **tone**.

Orff method: Music education that integrates language, music, and movement, emphasizing rhythm. Students use specially designed Orff percussion instruments and eventually recorders; developed by the German composer, teacher, and conductor Karl Orff (1859–1982).

phrase: An incomplete musical idea or short musical sentence.

phrasing: (1) Bringing out the phrases in proper relation to one another; (2) the musical symbols that show the performer how to accomplish this.

pianissimo: Very soft, written *pp*.

piano: Soft, written *p*.

pitch: The high to low quality of a musical sound, determined by the number of vibrations per second.

polyphony: The combination of two or more separate **melodies** to create a harmonious composition, from the Greek roots for "many voices."

prelude: A musical introduction to a composition or drama; sometimes an independent composition.

presto: Faster than **allegro.**

quartet: (1) A composition for four performers, for example, a string quartet or barbershop quartet; (2) the four performers collectively, for example, the Cleveland Quartet.

ragtime: A style of syncopated music, originated by African American composers, that was popular around the turn of the twentieth century.

repertoire: The compositions that a musician is prepared to perform.

rhythm: Anything pertaining to the duration of musical sounds.

ritardando, ritenuto (rit.): Slowing down.

rondo: A composition, usually with three parts, in which the first is repeated several times.

scales: An orderly series of **tones.** The scales that students learn first are the **major, minor,** and **chromatic.**

sharp: A character, ♯, that raises the following note a half **tone.**

sight-reading: The ability to play or sing music not previously seen.

solfège or **solfeggio**: A vocal exercise usually sung with do, re, mi, fa, sol.

sonata: (from *sonare,* to sound) A long instrumental composition. Sonatas are of a certain form consisting of three or four **movements** with contrasting themes, **tempos,** and moods, usually for a solo instrument or chamber ensemble.

sonatina: A short **sonata** with two or three **movements.**

soprano: The highest female or boy's voice.

staccato: Separated, distinct, or detached—the opposite of **legato.**

staff, stave: The five lines and the spaces between them, on which music is written.

stop: The part of the organ that admits and "stops" the flow of air.

Suzuki method: Music education that emphasizes an early start, parental participation, and playing by ear (reading music is added later). It focuses on playing an instrument rather than general music education; developed by Japanese violin teacher Shinichi Suzuki (1898–1998).

symphony: An instrumental composition for full orchestra in four **movements**.

syncopation: A shifting of the rhythmic accent to the normally unaccented part of the measure and sustaining the tone or tones into the normally accented part.

tempo: Time, rate of speed.

tenor: The highest natural adult male voice.

theory: The science of music, that is, the general rules of composing and arranging music.

time signature: A fraction written at the beginning of a composition or a section of a composition. The numerator indicates the number of beats per measure, and the denominator indicates the kind of note that gets one beat. For example, a waltz usually has the time signature 3/4, so that there are three beats to a measure and a quarter note has the value of one beat.

tone: A musical sound with a definite **pitch**.

tonic: The key or first note of any **scale**.

treble clef: The G clef, which rests on the second line of the **staff**.

trio: (1) A piece for three voices or instruments; (2) a three-person ensemble, for example, the Beaux Arts Trio; (3) a section of a **minuet, march**, or other composition.

triplets: A group of three notes played in the time assigned to two notes of the same value.

tuning: Adjusting an instrument to the right **pitch**. String instruments must be tuned each time they are played.

vibrato: A rapid, slight variation in pitch, usually in connection with vocal or string performance.

vivace: Lively and quick.

waltz: A dance, and the music for it, with three beats per **measure**, with the first beat accented.

Yamaha method: Music education for young children through group classes emphasizing ear training. It does not focus on instrumental performance. The Yamaha method was developed in the 1950s by a group of Japanese music teachers sponsored and inspired by Genichi Kawakami, chairman of the board of the Nippin Gakki and Yamaha companies.

n0tes

Preface

The Eleanor Roosevelt quote is from her column, "My Day," November 5, 1958, reprinted in *My Day*, ed. David Embledge (New York: Da Capo, 2001), p. 265.

Chapter 1

The John Adams quote is from his letter to his wife, Abigail, May 12, 1780, *Adams Family Correspondence*, vol. 3, p. 342. The quotations from Senators Hillary Clinton and Rick Santorum are taken from ". . . and Music for All," *American Music Teacher*, June–July 2002, p. 23.

Chapter 2

The studies discussed at the beginning of this chapter are: Frances Rauscher, Gordon L. Shaw, and K. N. Ky, "Music and Spatial Task Performance," *Nature* 365 (1993): 611; Rauscher, Shaw, and Ky, "Listening to Mozart Enhances Spatial-Temporal Reasoning," *Neuroscience Letters* 185 (1995): 44–47; Rauscher, Shaw, et al., "Music Training Causes Long-Term Enhancement of Preschool Children's Spatial-Temporal Reasoning Abilities," *Neurological Research* 19 (1997): 1–8; Rauscher and M. Zupan, "Classroom Keyboard Instruction Improves Kindergarten Children's Spatial-Temporal Performance: A Field Experiment," *Early Childhood Research Quarterly* 15 (2000): 215–28; Martin F. Gardiner, "Learning Improved by Arts Training," *Nature* 381 (1996): 284; Gardiner, "Music Learning and Behavior: A Case for Mental Stretching," *Journal for Learning Through Music*, 1 (2000): 72–93; I. Hurwitz, P. H. Wolff, B. D. Bortnick, and K. Kokas, "Nonmusical Effects of the Kodály Music Curriculum in Primary Grade Children," *Journal of Learning Disabilities* 8 (1975): 45–51; S. J. Lamb and A. H. Gregory, "The Relationship between Music and Reading in Beginning Readers," *Educational Psychology* 13 (1993): 19–26; N.

M. Weinberger, "Creating Creativity with Music," *MuSICA Research Notes* 5 (spring 1998): 1–5.

The summary from Stewart Gordon is from *Etudes for Piano Teachers* (New York: Oxford University Press, 1995), the quotations appear on pp. 135, 137, and 138. The Arnold Steinhardt quotations are from *Indivisible by Four* (New York: Farrar, Straus, and Giroax, 1998), pp. 20 and 32. The Charles Cooke quotation is from *Playing the Piano for Pleasure* (New York: Simon and Schuster, 1960), p. 42.

Chapter 3

The chapter epigraph is from Noah Adams, *Piano Lessons* (New York: Delacorte Press, 1996), p. 23. Alfred Brendel is quoted in David Dubal, *Reflections from the Keyboard*, 2d ed. (New York: Schirmer, 1997), p. 71. Information about Stephane Grappelli comes from Margaret Campbell, *The Great Violinists* (Garden City, N.Y.: Doubleday, 1981), pp. 202–3. Information about Jean-Pierre Rampal is from Pilar Estevan, *Talking with Flutists* (Edu-Tainment Publishing, 1976), p. 3. Yo-Yo Ma is quoted in David Blum, *Quintet: Five Journeys toward Musical Fulfillment* (Ithaca, N.Y.: Cornell University Press, 1999), p. 6. The quotation from Noah Adams comes from his *Piano Lessons*, pp. xviii–xix.

Chapter 4

The chapter epigraph is from Estevan, *Talking with Flutists*, p. 40. The Gregor Piatigorsky quotation is from his *Cellist* (Doubleday: Garden City, N.Y.: 1965), p. 5. Mstislav Rostropovich is quoted in Margaret Campbell, *The Great Cellists* (London: Victor Gollancz, 1988), p. 282. The stories about the anonymous eight-year-old and Artur Rubinstein are from Madeline Bruser, *The Art of Practicing: Making Music from the Heart* (New York: Bell Tower, 1999), p. 8; the Robert Casadesus quotation is from Dean Elder, *Pianists at Play* (London: Kahn and Averill, 1982), p. 28. The Charles Cooke quotation is from his *Playing the Piano for Pleasure*, p. 23.

Chapter 5

The chapter epigraph is from Mark Salzman's *The Soloist* (New York: Vintage, 1995), p. 181. The quotation from Josef Lhevinne is from his *Basic Principles in Pianoforte Playing* (1924; reprint, New York: Dover, 1972), chap. 3, p. 2. The quotation from Josef Hofmann is taken from his *Piano Playing: With Piano Questions Answered* (1909; reprint ed., New York: Dover, 1976), chap. 1, p. 2. The quotations from Arthur Schnabel are from his *My Life and Music* (1933, 1961; reprint, New York: Dover, 1988), p. 211.

Chapter 6

Arthur Schnabel is quoted from *My Life*, p. 163. Ivan Galamian is quoted in Campbell, *Great Violinists*, p. 273. The Hofmann quotation is from his *Piano Playing*, pp. 48–49. The story about Arnold Steinhardt comes from his *Indivisible by Four*, p. 33.

Chapter 7

The chapter epigraph is from the entry Competitions in Music 1. Introductory in *The Oxford Companion to Music*, 10th edition (New York: Oxford University Press, 1970), p. 213. The Steinhardt quotations are from *Indivisible by Four*, pp. 32 and 37. Alfred Brendel is quoted in Dubal, *Reflections from the Keyboard*, p. 72. The Mark Salzman quotation is from his novel *The Soloist*, pp. 268–69. The Madeline Bruser quotation is from *The Art of Practicing*, p. 228. The Josef Hofmann quotation is from *Piano Playing*, pp. 121–22. Vladimir Ashkenazy, Alicia de Larrocha, and Vladimir Horowitz are quoted in Uszler, Gordon, and Mach, *Well-Tempered Keyboard Teacher*, p. 371.

Chapter 8

The chapter epigraph is from Steinhardt, *Indivisible by Four*, p. 10. Robert Schumann is quoted in Steinhardt, *Indivisible by Four*, p. 78. Paula Robison is quoted in Estevan, *Talking with Flutists*, p. 41.

Chapter 9

The chapter epigraph is from Hoffman, *Piano Playing*, p. 132–33. The Josef Hofmann quotation also is from *Piano Playing*, pp. 132–33. Doriot Dwyer is quoted in Estevan, *Talking with Flutists*, pp. 51–52.

Chapter 10

The chapter epigraph is from Judith Kogan, *Nothing but the Best: The Struggle for Perfection at the Juilliard School* (New York: Limelight, 1989), p. 45. Gina Bachauer is quoted in Elder, *Pianists*, p. 92. Yehudi Menuhin is quoted in Campbell, *Great Violinists*, p. 231. Alfred Brendel is quoted in Dubal, *Reflections from the Keyboard*, p. 71. David Denby tells the story of Rachel Lee in "Prodigious," *The New Yorker*, October 18 and 25, 1999, p. 174. The quote about travel is from Kogan, *Nothing but the Best*, p. 46. The Arnold Steinhardt quotes are from *Indivisible by Four*, pp. 6, 65–66. Lynn Harrell is quoted in Campbell, *The Great Cellists*, p. 314. Julius Baker is quoted in Estevan, *Talking with Flutists*, pp. 16–17, 39. The discussion of success is quoted from Stewart Gordon, *Etudes for Piano Teachers*, pp. 28–29. Gordon's later description of music's role in life comes from p. 30. Gina Bachauer is quoted in Adele Marcus, *Great Pianists Speak with Adele Marcus* (Neptune, N.J.: Paganiniana, 1979), p. 17. Isaac Stern's comments on Yo-Yo Ma come from Blum, *Quintet*, p. 14. Jane Bowyer Stewart described the importance of her liberal arts education in the *Phi Beta Kappa Key Reporter* (winter 2000–01), p. 4. The Ignace Paderewski quotation is from Cooke, *Playing the Piano for Pleasure*, p. 25. Paula Robison is quoted in Estevan, *Talking with Flutists*, pp. 16–17. Leon Fleisher is quoted in Marienne Uszler, Stewart Gordon, and Elyse Mach, *The Well-Tempered Keyboard Teacher* (New York: Schirmer, 1991), p. 385.

for further information

Books for Children

(books marked with an asterisk are suitable for younger children)

Activities

*Drew, Helen. *My First Music Book*. New York: Dorling Kindersley, 1993.

*Dunleavy, Deborah. *The Kids Can Press Jumbo Book of Music*. Tonawanda, N.Y.: Kids Can Press, 2001.

Hopkin, Bart. *Making Simple Musical Instruments: A Melodious Collection of Strings, Winds, Drums, and More*. Asheville, NC: Lark Books, 1995.

*Walther, Tom. *Make More Music!* Boston: Little, Brown, 1981.

Waring, Dennis. *Cool Cardboard Instruments to Make and Play*. Winnipeg, Canada: Tamos Books, 2000.

*Wiseman, Ann. *Making Musical Things*. New York: Scribner, 1979.

Biography

*Anderson, M. T. *Handel: Who Knew What He Liked*. Boston: Candlewick, 2001.

George-Warren, Holly. *Shake, Rattle, and Roll: The Founders of Rock & Roll*. Boston: Houghton Mifflin, 2001.

Krull, Kathleen. *Lives of the Musicians: Good Times, Bad Times (and What the Neighbors Thought)*. New York: Harcourt Brace Jovanovich, 1993.

Lester, Julius. *The Blues Singers: Ten Who Rocked the World*. New York: Hyperion, 2001.

Monceaux, Morgan. *Jazz: My Music, My People*. New York: Knopf, 1994.

Mour, Stanley. *American Jazz Musicians*. Berkeley Heights, N.J.: Ensslow, 1998.

*Nichol, Barbara. *Beethoven Lives Upstairs*. New York: Orchard, 1999. CD also available.

Rachlin, Ann, and Susan Hellard. Famous Children series. London: Gollancz, 1992– . Includes biographies of Bach, Beethoven, Brahms, Chopin, Handel, Haydn, Mozart, Schubert, Schumann, and Tchaikovsky.

Tate, Eleanora E. *African American Musicians*. New York: John Wiley & Sons, 2000.

Venezia, Mike. Getting to Know the World's Composers series. Includes volumes on Bach, Beethoven, Bernstein, Gershwin, Handel, Mozart, and Tchaikovsky.

Vernon, Roland. Introducing . . . series. Parsippany, N.J.: Silver Burdett, 1996– . Includes volumes on Bach, Chopin, Gershwin, Mozart, Stravinsky, Verdi, and Vivaldi.

Careers

Blackwood, Alan. *The Performing World of the Singer*. Parsippany, N.J.: Silver Burdett, 1981.

Greenspoon, Jaq. *Career Portraits: Music*. Lincolnwood, Ill.: VGM Career Horizons, 1995.

Headington, Christopher. *The Performing World of the Musician*. Parsippany, N.J.: Silver Burdett, 1981.

Lee, Barbara. *Working in Music*. Minneapolis, Minn.: Lerner Publications, 1996.

*Paxton, Arthur K. *Making Music*. New York: Atheneum, 1986.

Reeves, Diane Lindsey, with Gayle Bryan. *Career Ideas for Kids Who Like Music and Dance*. New York: Facts on File, 2001.

Wolff, Virginia E. *The Mozart Season*. New York: Henry Holt, 1991. A young adult novel.

General Information and Reference

Ardley, Neil. *A Young Person's Guide to Music*. New York: Dorling Kindersley, 1995. With CD.

Barber, Nicola, and Mary Mure. *The World of Music*. Parsippany, N.J.: Silver Burdett, 1996.

Berger, Melvin. *The Science of Music*. New York: Crowell, 1989.

*Blackwood, Alan. *Musical Instruments*. New York: Bookwright, 1987.

*Chesky, David. *Classical Cats: A Children's Introduction to the Orchestra*. Chesky Records, 1997. Book and CD.

*Elliott, Donald. *Alligators and Music*. Boston: Gambit, 1976.

*Ganesi, Anita. *The Young Person's Guide to the Orchestra: Benjamin Britten's Composition*. New York: Harcourt, 1996. Book and CD.

*Hayes, Ann. *Meet the Orchestra*. New York: Harcourt Brace Jovanovich, 1991. A Reading Rainbow book.

*Koscielniak, Bruce. *The Story of the Incredible Orchestra: An Introduction to Musical Instruments and the Symphony Orchestra*. Boston: Houghton Mifflin, 2000.

Live Music Series. New York: Thomson Learning, 1993– . Volumes on brass, keyboards, percussion, strings, the voice, and woodwinds.

*McLeish, Kenneth and Valerie. *The Oxford First Companion to Music*. New York: Oxford University Press, 1982.

Nathan, Amy. *The Young Musician's Survival Guide: Tips from Teens and Pros*. New York: Oxford University Press, 2000.

Scholes, Percy A. *The Oxford Junior Companion to Music*. New York: Oxford University Press, 1974.

Spence, Keith. *The Young People's Book of Music*. Brookfield, Conn.: Millbrook, 1993.

*Weil, Lisl. *The Magic of Music*. New York: Holiday House, 1989.

Opera and Ballet

*Blyth, Alan. *Cinderella (La Cenerentola): The Story of Rossini's Opera*. New York: Franklin Watts, 1981.

*Geras, Adèle. Magic of Ballet series. Devon, U.K.: David and Charles. Volumes to date include *Giselle, Swan Lake*, and *The Nutcracker*.

*———. *The Random House Book of Opera Stories*. New York: Random House, 1997.

*Greaves, Margaret. *The Magic Flute: The Story of Mozart's Opera*. New York: Henry Holt, 1989.

*Husain, Shahrukh. *The Barefoot Book of Stories from the Opera*. New York: Barefoot Books, 1999.

*Spruyt, E. Lee. *Behind the Golden Curtain: Hansel and Gretel at the Great Opera House*. New York: Four Winds, 1986.

Picture Books and Preschool Videos

*Baby Einstein series. Videos include *Baby Bach* and *Baby Mozart*; CDs include *Baby Bach, Baby Mozart, Animal Classics* (including music from popular children's cartoons), *Bedtime Classics*, and *Holiday Classics*. Nonmusic products, including the *Baby Einstein* and *Baby Newton* videos, use classical music as well. All videos and CDs in the series are designed for children from birth to three.

*Celenza, Anna Harwell. *The Farewell Symphony*. Watertown, Mass.: Charlesbridge, 2000. With CD.

*Cutler, Jane. *The Cello of Mr. O*. New York: Dutton, 1999.

*Deetlefs, Rene. *The Song of Six Birds*. New York: Dutton, 1999.

*Dengler, Marianna. *Fiddlin' Sam*. Flagstaff, Ariz.: Rising Moon, 1999.

*Fleischman, Paul. *Rondo in C*. New York: Harper & Row, 1988.

*Fleming, Candace. *Gabriella's Song*. New York: Atheneum, 1997.

*Hurd, Thacher. *Mama Don't Allow*. New York: Harper & Row, 1984. A Reading Rainbow book.

*Igus, Toyomi, and Michele Wood. *I See the Rhythm*. San Francisco: Children's Book Press, 1998.

*Karlins, Mark. *Music over Manhattan*. New York: Doubleday, 1998.

*Kuskin, Karla. *The Philharmonic Gets Dressed*. New York: Harper & Row, 1986.

*Les Chats Pelés. *Long Live Music!* Mankato, Minn. Creative Editions, 1996.

*Martin, Bill, Jr. *The Maestro Plays*. New York: Henry Holt, 1994.

*McPhail, David. *Mole Music*. New York: Henry Holt, 1999.

*Medearis, Angela. *The Singing Man*. New York: Holiday House, 1994.

*Millman, Isaac. *Moses Goes to a Concert*. New York: Farrar Straus and Giroux, 1998.

*Moss, Lloyd. *Zin! Zin! Zin!: A Violin*. New York: Simon & Schuster, 1995. A Caldecott Honor book.

*Pinkney, J. Brian. *Max Found Two Stones*. New York: Aladdin, 1997. A Reading Rainbow book.

*Takao, Yuku. *A Winter Concert*. Brookfield, Conn.: Millbrook, 1995.

*Turner, Barrie Carson. *Carnival of the Animals*. New York: Henry Holt, 1998. With CD.

The Wiggles. *The Wiggles Series*. An Australian quartet performs folk/pop songs and dances for toddlers. Video, DVD.

Recordings for Children and Parents

This list represents a mere selection from hundreds of possibilities that you can find in your music store or on the Web. There are numerous recordings of lullabies, Disney tunes, film scores, Broadway shows, nursery rhymes, rock albums for kids, and folk music from around the world. Any of your favorite recordings are fine, but this list provides a good starting point for those unfamiliar with classical music.

Beethoven Lives Upstairs. Classical Kids. A musical biography.

Bibbidi, Bobbidi, Bach: More Favorite Disney Tunes in the Style of Great Classic Composers. Delos.

Build Your Baby's Brain through the Power of Music. Sony. A series of classical recordings for children with a variety of composers and performers.

Classical Baby. GAA.

The Classical Child: Early to Rise. Sophia Sounds.

Classics for Children. Decca Records.

Classics for Kids. Arthur Fiedler, The Boston Pops, and others; RCA Victor.

Heigh-Ho! Mozart: Favorite Disney Tunes in the Style of Great Classic Composers. Delos.

Introducing Music of the World. Putumayo. Two CDs.

Listen, Learn, and Grow. Naxos. A series that includes playtime activities for ages two through seven, lullabies, and music for infants.

Mad About Kids' Classics: The Greatest Music from Disney Cartoons. Deutsche Grammophon.

The Mozart Effect. Don Campbell; Atlantic Records. CDs for expectant mothers, newborns, babies, and children.

Mozart's Magic Fantasy. Classical Kids.

Sweet Dreams. CBS Records.

Sweet Dreams. Delta. Two CDs.

The Ultimate Wizard Album. Decca Records. Great works inspired by the world of fantasy, magic, and imagination.

Ultra Sound. James Galway, The Boston Pops, André Previn; RCA Victor. Classical works for expectant mothers and unborn children.

Vivaldi's Ring of Mystery. Atlantic Classical Kids.

Books, Websites, and Organizations for Parents

As your children learn about music, these resources for adults will be helpful and, we hope, enjoyable.

Activities

Kleiner, Lynn. *Babies Make Music!: For Parents and Their Babies*. New York: Warner, 2000.

____. *Toddlers Make Music! Ones and Twos!: For Parents and Their Toddlers*. New York: Warner, 2000.

Careers

Horowitz, Joseph. *The Ivory Trade: Piano Competitions and the Business of Music*. Boston: Northeastern University Press, 1990.

Kogan, Judith. *Nothing but the Best: The Struggle for Perfection at the Juilliard School*. New York: Limelight, 1989.

Catalogues

The most inclusive catalogue for musical books, toys, CDs, and more is *Music in Motion* (www.musicmotion.com; 800-445-0649; P.O. Box 869231, Plano, TX, 75086); includes games, basic rhythm instruments for children, Orff instruments, instruments from around the world, recorders, posters, stickers, software, and videos.

Dictionaries

Kennedy, Michael, and Joyce Bourne, eds. *Concise Oxford Dictionary of Music.* New York: Oxford University Press, 1996.

Randel, Don Michael, ed. *New Harvard Dictionary of Music.* Cambridge: Harvard University Press, 1986.

Slonimsky, Nicolas, et al. *Schirmer Pronouncing Pocket Manual of Musical Terms.* 5th ed. New York: Schirmer, 2002.

Educational Organizations

American Orff-Schulwerk Association, Box 391089, Cleveland, OH 44139-8089; 440-543-5366; www.aosa.org; provides information on the Orff method, local chapters, grants, and scholarships.

American String Teachers Association, 4135 Chain Bridge Road, Fairfax, VA 22030; 703-729-2113; fax 703-279-2114; www.astaweb.com; the website offers information on programs and competitions, a list of state chapters for teacher referrals, and information on student chapters and membership.

Music Teachers National Association, 441 Vine Street, Suite 505, Cincinnati, OH 45202-2811; 888-512-5278; 513-421-1420; fax 513-421-2503; www.mtna.org; offers student competitions and online teacher referrals.

Music Together, 66 Witherspoon Avenue, Princeton, NJ 08542; 800-728-2692; www.musictogether.com; a program for infant through prekindergarten children for use at home or in preschools. The website provides information on the curriculum, materials, and classes available nationwide.

National Association for Music Education, 1806 Robert Fulton Drive, Reston, VA 20191; 800-336-3768; 703-860-4000; www.menc.org; offers advocacy information to help parents promote music in the schools as well as information on festivals, scholarships, and careers.

National Association of Teachers of Singing, 2800 North University Boulevard, Jacksonville, FL 32211; 904-744-9022; www.nats.org; offers student auditions, competitions, workshops, recitals, and master classes. The website allows an online search for teachers by location and style of music.

National Piano Foundation, 13140 Coit Road, Suite 320, LB 120, Dallas, TX 75240-5737; 972-233-9107; fax 972-490-4219; www.pianonet.com; write or call for a list of brochures and videos.

Organization of American Kodály Educators, 1612 29th Avenue S., Moorhead, MN 56560; 218-227-6253; fax 218-227-6254; www.oake.org; website provides information on summer programs, state chapters, and a chat room.

Suzuki Association of the Americas, Box 17310, Boulder, CO 80308; 303-444-0948; fax 303-444-0984; www.suzukiassociation.org; website provides information on the Suzuki method, membership, summer institutes, and teacher referrals.

Yamaha International Music Education, 6600 Orangethorpe Avenue, Buena Park, CA 90522; 800-722-8856; www.yamaha.com; website provides a description of the Yamaha program, a directory of participating music schools, a bulletin board, and a directory of Yamaha summer programs.

Guides to Summer Programs and Colleges

Directory of Summer Music Programs. Tacoma, WA: Music Resources Press, 2000.

Everett, Carole J. *The Performing Arts Major's College Guide.* New York: Arco, 1998.

Muriel Topaz et al., *Guide to Performing Arts Programs: Profiles of over Six Hundred Colleges, High Schools, and Summer Programs.* New York: Princeton Review Press, 1998.

These directories are useful but quickly become outdated. You can supplement them with a Web search on "summer music programs," which will yield hundreds of possibilities. These range from week-long day camps for young children to highly selective residential programs open to accomplished young people who must audition for places. Your child's private music teacher or the music teacher at your child's school will have suggestions about nearby programs. Another likely source of information is the music department of a nearby college, university, or conservatory. Ask for complete information and, if possible, talk with the parents of former students. Many of these programs offer scholarships.

More about Music

Adams, Noah. *Piano Lessons: Music, Love, and True Adventures.* New York: Delacorte, 1996.

Bernstein, Leonard. *The Joy of Music.* New York: Doubleday Anchor, 1994.

Blum, David. *Quintet: Five Journeys toward Musical Fulfillment.* Ithaca, N.Y.: Cornell University Press, 1999.

Carhart, Thad. *The Piano Shop on the Left Bank: Discovering a Forgotten Passion in a Paris Atelier.* New York: Random House, 2001.

Cooke, Charles. *Playing the Piano for Pleasure.* New York: Simon and Schuster, 1960.

Copland, Aaron. *What to Listen for in Music.* New York: Penguin, 1999.

Haas, Karl. *Inside Music: How to Understand, Listen to, and Enjoy Good Music.* New York: Doubleday Anchor, 1984.

Hoffman, Miles. *The NPR Classical Music Companion: Terms and Concepts from A to Z.* Boston: Houghton Mifflin, 1997.

Latham, Alison, ed. *The Oxford Companion to Music.* New York: Oxford University Press, 2002.

Lee, Don, ed. *The NPR Basic Record Library: A Classical CD Guide from Performance Today.* Washington, D.C.: National Public Radio, 1999.

Libbey, Ted. *The NPR Guide to Building a Classical CD Collection.* New York: Workman, 1999.

Rothstein, Edward. *Emblems of Mind: The Inner Life of Music and Mathematics.* New York: Avon, 1995.

Salzman, Mark. *The Soloist.* New York: Vintage, 1995.

Schonberg, Harold C. *The Lives of the Great Composers.* 3d ed. New York: Norton, 1997.

Steinhardt, Arnold. *Indivisible by Four.* New York: Farrar, Straus and Giroux, 1998.

Waring, Dennis. *Great Wood Folk Instruments to Make and Play.* New York: Sterling Publishing, 1999.

Special Needs

American Music Therapy Association, 8455 Colesville Road, Suite 1000, Silver Spring, MD 20910; 301-589-3300; fax 301-589-5175; www.musictherapy.org; provides information on careers and education for music therapy and will provide teacher referrals in response to a mail or email request: (findMT@musictherapy.org)

Roland, David. *The Confident Performer.* Boston: Heinemann, 1998.

Streeter, Elaine. *Making Music with the Young Child with Special Needs: A Guide for Parents.* London: Kingsley, 1994.

VSA Arts. 1300 Connecticut Avenue, N.W., Suite 700, Washington, D.C. 20036; 800-933-8721; TDD 202-737-0645; fax 202-737-0725; www.vsarts.org; arts activities and education for people with disabilities; teacher resource guides; prizes.

index